THE
GREAT CANADIAN
COTTAGE BOOK

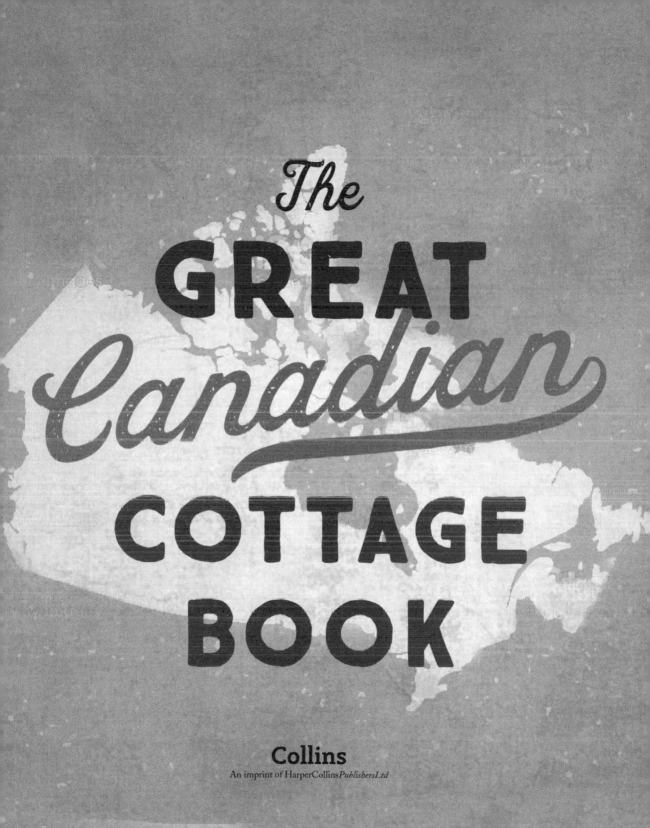

The
GREAT
Canadian
COTTAGE
BOOK

Collins
An imprint of HarperCollins*PublishersLtd*

The Great Canadian Cottage Book
Copyright © 2023 by HarperCollins Canada.

Published by Collins, an imprint of HarperCollins Publishers Ltd

First edition

Portions of this book have been published previously in the following HarperCollins publications: *Canadian Courage: True Stories of Canada's Everyday Heroes* by Linda Pruessen (2021); *The Great Canadian Cottage Puzzle Book* (2015); *The Great Canadian Holiday Puzzle Book* (2015); *The Great Canadian Road Trip Puzzle Book* (2015); and *Class Clown Joke Book* (2020).

This publication contains the opinions and ideas of its author(s) and is designed to provide useful advice in regard to the subject matter covered. This publication is not intended to provide a basis for action in particular circumstances without consideration by a competent professional. The author(s) and publisher expressly disclaim any responsibility for any liability, loss, or risk, personal or otherwise, which is incurred as a consequence, directly or indirectly, of the use and application of any of the contents of this book.

Excerpts from *The Camping Cookbook* by Heather Thomas on pp. 33–38, 40–55 and 150–51 © HarperCollins*Publishers* 2021. Reprinted by permission of HarperCollins Publishers Ltd.

Interior illustrations: Shutterstock.

HarperCollins books may be purchased for educational, business, or sales promotional use through our Special Markets Department.

HarperCollins Publishers Ltd
Bay Adelaide Centre, East Tower
22 Adelaide Street West, 41st Floor
Toronto, Ontario, Canada
M5H 4E3

www.harpercollins.ca

Library and Archives Canada Cataloguing in Publication

Title: The great Canadian cottage book.
Identifiers: Canadiana (print) 20230141633 Canadiana (ebook) 20230141641 | ISBN 9781443470667 (softcover) | ISBN 9781443470674 (EPUB)
Subjects: LCSH: Country life—Anecdotes. | LCSH: Family recreation—Miscellanea. | LCSH: Outdoor life—Anecdotes. | LCSH: Outdoor recreation—Miscellanea. | LCSH: Vacation homes—Canada. | LCSH: Cottages—Canada. | LCGFT: Anecdotes. | LCGFT: Trivia and miscellanea.
Classification: LCC GV191.44 .G74 2023 | DDC 796.50971—dc23

Printed and bound in the United States of America
23 24 25 26 27 LBC 5 4 3 2 1

"DO YOU THINK WE'LL BEAT THE TRAFFIC?"

—Hopeful on the Highway

CONTENTS

A COTTAGE
BY ANY OTHER NAME . . .

In the summertime, do you go to your cottage or to your cabin? Or maybe you go to a camp? Well, it all depends on where you live. In fact, what Canadians call their summer homes may just be the most regionally varied term across the country.

Residents of southern Ontario and most parts of the Maritime provinces prefer *cottage* to describe their weekend retreats. In the west, especially British Columbia, *cabin* reigns supreme. That's also the favoured term in Newfoundland and Labrador.

Although *cottage* and *cabin* are the most popular variations by far, in some areas of the country you're more likely to hear other names. *Chalet* is a popular choice in Quebec, while Manitobans might "go to the lake" for the weekend. In northern Ontario and parts of New Brunswick, a summer residence is called a *camp*. And one interesting variation is found only on Cape Breton Island, where *bungalow* is the word of choice for a vacation home.

No matter what you call it, I think we can all agree on one thing: the next best thing to having a summer place is having a good friend with a summer place. Don't forget to pack insect repellent!

"WAS THAT OUR EXIT?"

—Better Late than Never

Campfire Stories

HIDDEN AWAY IN THE COUNTRY

*The case of the vanishing cabin went from baffling to messy
as police tried to figure out whether a crime had even been committed.*

In June 2022, in Saskatchewan, CTV News reported that a house had gone missing. It was being moved from Tisdale, a little town about 200 kilometres northeast of Saskatoon. The house was a small wooden bungalow, and it had been lifted onto a trailer for transport by truck. Around midnight on June 14, someone took it. The house was gone.

The Royal Canadian Mounted Police investigated and learned of a disagreement between the owner of the home and a thirty-two-year-old man, "Sam." The previous day, the men had had an "altercation." It seemed obvious who had spirited the house away. Police charged Sam with theft. They also charged him with uttering threats and assault with a weapon. A court date was set.

The only thing the Mounties couldn't figure out was what he'd done with the house.

A house isn't the smartest thing to steal. Obviously, you can't live in a stolen house—the theft will be discovered as soon as anyone visits. It seemed that Sam was not much good as a criminal, although he might have a bright future as a magician.

As of this writing, the house mystery remains unsolved, but perhaps the RCMP can draw some clues from a similar case in Oregon, in 2015. There, too, a residence went missing from a very isolated area about 60 kilometres from Klamath Falls. And if you've never heard of Klamath Falls, it's a small town about 450 kilometres south of Portland. We're talking "out of the way." In this case, the missing structure was a 1,500-square-foot log cabin, complete with deck. The owner turned up one day to find an empty lot—the foundation was there, but the cabin was gone.

The local police had never come across a case like it. They scoured the area and found signs that the house had been jacked up and moved on a truck. They talked with neighbors and informants, but it was finally the department's "forest unit" (we're imagining cartoon animals) who solved the case—the cabin's new location was about a kilometre from its original site. In fact, if someone had thought to stand on the old lot and gaze across the large meadow behind it, they might have spied the cabin through the distant trees.

It seemed like the cabin snatcher was the most audacious thief in Oregon—either that, or he had logs for brains. But when police talked to the occupant, it turned out that he wasn't a thief at all, and the situation was complicated.

The man who had arranged for the cabin to be moved had bought it in good faith from another man who claimed to own it. That's because three different people had their names on the title to the cabin—the man who had reported its absence, his ex-girlfriend, and her ex-husband. The ex-girlfriend had reconciled with the ex-husband, and her ex-boyfriend moved away. Later, without informing the other owners, the now "*ex*-ex-husband" sold the cabin to an unsuspecting buyer, who hired a company to remove the cabin he'd purchased and shifted it to his own property.

The case of the vanishing cabin went from baffling to messy as police tried to figure out whether a crime had even been committed by the seller, whether the cabin's former owners needed to sort out their disagreements in a civil court, and who was still an "ex" of who.

DIVING IN THE DARK

"You'll never see a dive like this again, that's for sure."
—ERIK BROWN

On a normal day, Thailand's Tham Luang Nang Non cave system isn't particularly difficult to navigate—which explains its popularity with the local Wild Boar soccer team. The seventeen-year-olds and their coach enjoyed exploring the complex under the mountain range that straddles the Thailand–Myanmar border. So it was nothing out of the ordinary when the twelve teammates and their coach decided to head to the caves on June 23, 2018, carrying nothing more than flashlights. They weren't planning to be there for long. But a monsoon blew in, bringing with it torrential rains and massive flooding. The team became trapped, and the search and rescue mission began.

Erik Brown, a Canadian from Langley, British Columbia, had just returned to his dive shop in Koh Tao, about four hundred kilometres south of Tham Luang, when he heard about the rescue efforts and reached out to a friend involved to see if divers were needed. They were, so Erik and another friend were on a plane the next morning. "If they need help, and there's anything I can do, I'm going," he said in a phone call to his mother.

Erik's first dive was on a trip to Australia in 2004. He fell in love. In the years that followed, he received certification in various disciplines, including deep diving, technical diving, and cave diving. In 2010, he moved to Egypt and co-founded a technical diving school— Team Blue Immersion (TBI)—near the Red Sea's infamous "Blue Hole," one of the most dangerous diving spots in the world. They offered training seminars, completed world-record dives, and provided logistics services for documentaries. In August 2013, Erik was part of Expedition Alexander Hamilton, a dangerous mission nearly a hundred metres underwater off the coast of Iceland. They placed a memorial plaque on the first American ship sunk during the Second World War.

For divers with Erik's training and experience, cave rescues are part of the work, although the results are often grim. "Ninety percent of the stuff I go out on unfortunately on these occasions is [body recovery]," he says. As Erik headed north towards Tham Luang, he hoped that this time would be different. But the early days of the Thai search and rescue mission didn't offer much reason for optimism.

On Sunday, June 24, a crew located the boys' bags and sandals, but rising waters forced them to suspend the search. The following day, a team of Thai Royal Navy SEALs reached an inner cave, where they found handprints on the wall. Again, flooding sent them back. By Sunday, July 1, Thai army and navy troops had been joined by local volunteers as well as rescue specialists from the United States, the United Kingdom, China, and Australia. Efforts to pump water out of the caves were well under way, with additional heavy-duty equipment being flown in by plane. But so far, it had all been for naught. As the world watched and waited, hopes for a successful rescue began to fade.

The breakthrough came on Monday, July 2, when British divers John Volanthen and Rick Stanton managed to make their way through the tunnels and caves—nearly half of which required diving in treacherous conditions—to the ledge where the boys and their coach were perched. They had been in the cave for nine days.

July 2 was also the day that Erik arrived, just as efforts swung into full "rescue" mode. The first priority was bringing fresh water, food, blankets, and medical supplies to the boys, whose coach had taught them to meditate as a to stay calm and preserve oxygen. At one point, the rescuers hoped to bring oxygen tanks to the team, but on Friday, July 6, Saman Kunan, a former Thai SEAL, died when his own tank ran out. The tunnels were too narrow. The only option was to get the boys out.

Erik knew it wouldn't be easy. "Every single challenge you can throw at a diver was there," he says. Zero visibility, long hikes in, super-narrow channels, no communication between divers, and long stretches of passages and by-passages with quick currents all contributed to the extreme conditions.

The rescue team devised an elaborate system for bringing the team out. Since the cave conditions made a buddy system with two divers impossible, an oxygen cylinder would be strapped to the front of the boy and a handle attached to his back. Then he would be outfitted with a full face mask and clipped to a diver who swam behind. The teams would have to squeeze through cracks, sometimes only 30 centimetres wide, and find their way through the dark passages by holding on to dive lines that had been laid ahead of time.

Even for an experienced diver like Erik, it was a daring operation. "When I arrived here and went in the first dive and saw even the first section, which is the twenty-five-minute underwater swim and navigation through pretty much mud . . . I won't lie—in my head I was [thinking] there's very little chance this would work," Erik says.

On Sunday, July 8, the oxygen levels in the cave were dangerously low. It was time to start bringing the boys out. Support divers were stationed along the route with fresh oxygen tanks, ready to assist those travelling with the boys, who were sedated to keep them calm during the ordeal.

Erik was positioned a few hours into the cave in the almost total darkness. "When they say zero visibility, they mean zero visibility—you can't see anything." In a message home to his family, he described the diving as like "swimming in coffee." He was unable to communicate with any of the divers moving in what seemed like slow motion around him. For hours at a time, he knew only what was happening in his small section of the cave.

"So you're not really sure how successful it is," he says. "It was successful up to me but they still had two hours to get [out]." Each shift lasted about ten hours, and staying calm was sometimes a challenge. Erik had to turn his "brain off a little bit." He says, "You have to focus on the minor task you have, try to put the sort of grand scale off to the side a little bit. Nothing prepares you for something like this. You'll never see a dive like this again, that's for sure."

Over the course of three days—July 8, 9, and 10—and against all odds, the rescuers safely brought out all twelve boys and their coach. On his Facebook page, Erik shared a photo of himself with two other divers, with the caption: "9 days, 7 missions, and 63 hours inside. Success."

Afterward, Erik found himself interviewed by news outlets from Canada and around the world. And back home in British Columbia, he received the Silver Medal for Bravery from the lieutenant-governor. Now, he cherishes the memories and the friends he made during those days in the caves. "You literally couldn't write this. It's extraordinary what some of these guys pulled off, and I'm happy that I could help in whatever way I could."

CAMPFIRE STORIES

THE OLDEST STORY IN THE SKY

Can it be just a coincidence that parallel tales emerged among people on opposite sides of the world about the same nondescript points of light in the sky?

One of the pleasures of the countryside is enjoying the night sky—a black sky, unspoiled by city lights, decorated with countless white stars, looking more or less the same today as they have looked for thousands of years. But in some cases, the subtle movements of the stars can reveal secrets about our own history.

Near the constellation of Orion, you might recognize the star cluster known as the Seven Sisters, or Pleiades. You can find it by drawing a line from the belt of Orion upwards. The Pleiades is a tight cluster of tiny stars looking a little like a miniature Big Dipper.

The cluster's name comes from ancient Greek mythology. The Pleiades were seven sisters, the daughters of Pleione, a minor goddess who protected sailors. Their father is a little more famous—he was Atlas, the Titan who held the earth on his shoulders. The seven maidens were particularly beautiful, and one day they caught the lascivious eye of the hunter Orion. He knew their father was preoccupied holding up the world, so he chased them. The gods intervened—changing the sisters into doves and then stars, and sending a scorpion (the constellation Scorpio) to sting Orion as a punishment. Every night Orion chases the seven sisters across the sky, while he is pursued by the scorpion.

Of course, this is just one myth among many. People all over the world can see the cluster, and many other cultures have their own stories about these stars. But many of these stories are strangely similar. For example, an ancient Huron legend also sees the stars as seven sisters—star maidens who visited earth. And, just as in the Greek legend, the sisters were chased by a hunter. In the Huron version, the hunter was a human who had fallen in love with one of the maidens.

Similar stories are told across cultures separated by thousands of miles and countless centuries. Australian Aboriginal culture was isolated from other parts of the world for 50,000 years, yet even in the remote western desert of Australia, an Aboriginal story, passed down for millennia, describes a tale similar to the one told by the Greeks—that the same cluster represents seven girls running from a lustful man named Nyiru. He too is represented by a constellation, corresponding to Orion.

Can it be just a coincidence that parallel tales emerged among people on opposite sides of the world about the same nondescript points of light in the sky? One explanation might be that the stories all come from a common source, passed down through word of mouth, but this seems hard to believe—if these stories share a common origin, it must date far back into ancient prehistory. And yet there is another curious piece of evidence suggesting that's exactly what happened.

One common element of the Seven Sisters legend is the number of stars mentioned—seven. But the average person gazing at the cluster will see six stars, not seven. Of course, through a telescope, astronomers can see hundreds of stars in this group, but most are very faint. Only six are bright enough to be distinguished with the naked eye. So why do we call these stars "the seven sisters" and not "the six sisters"?

The ancient Greeks had the same problem. Their story was about seven sisters, but they too saw only six stars.

In their tales, they claimed there was a lost sister. The story says that six of the Pleiades sisters were partnered with gods and bore their children, but the seventh, Merope, left the heavens to marry a human king, and her star faded away.

This detail of a seventh sister, a missing star, is also found in other cultures. For example, the Nez Perce people of the Pacific Northwest say the stars were once seven sisters, but one sister fell in love with a man who died, and she was so stricken with grief that she pulled the sky over her face as a veil.

Even in cultures where the stars don't represent seven sisters, but may be seven children, or seven chicks, the story often explains how the seventh member disappeared. In Japan, the constellation is known as Subaru and is said to represent seven stars, although only six are visible. The logo of the Subaru car company shows the six visible stars. A Cherokee myth says the stars are seven brothers. They played instead of working and rose up into the heavens. Their mother grabbed the seventh and pulled him back to earth, leaving only six in the sky.

You might wonder if these ancient myths about a disappearing seventh star reflect a real astronomical event. Is it possible that this group of six bright stars once contained a seventh member that is now invisible? Astronomers wondered this too. Using the Gaia space telescope, they made careful measurements of the almost imperceptible movements of the stars as they swirl around the cluster. Today, two stars in the cluster are so close together that they appear as one—what astronomers call an "optical binary"—but these stars have slowly changed position over the millennia and were once further apart than they appear today. So, how far back would you have to go before these stars appeared as two distinct points to the naked eye? The astronomers did some calculations and were astonished by the answer. The Seven Sisters were last visible as seven distinct stars around 100,000 years ago.

If the story of the Seven Sisters is really that old, it may solve the mystery of how the tale has spread so widely, because 100,000 years ago, there were no humans in Greece or America or Siberia or Australia. The ancestors of every human on earth were all still living in Africa, and apparently sharing the same stories.

As our species spread out from Africa and migrated around the world, we may have taken this story with us, and although it has changed, it has endured from that time to this, through all those millennia and through countless civilizations in history and prehistory.

When you look up into the night sky at the Seven Sisters, you are enjoying a sight viewed by your ancient forebears, and you are connected to the stories they told.

THE SCREAMING TUNNEL

One night, the girl left her bedroom.
In the kitchen, she found a box of matches.

The Bruce Trail is the longest hiking trail in Canada, and it's full of natural wonders. But if you follow the Bruce Trail from Niagara Falls to St. Catharines, you may come across one of the country's most famous supernatural wonders: the Screaming Tunnel. The tunnel lies near the end of a country road, not far from a busy highway, yet even by day, it has a sinister quality—in the midst of a grassy hill, a stone archway leads into darkness. A mess of graffiti surrounds the entrance. This feels like a place that might be the site of a murder scene, and it was used as such in David Cronenberg's 1982 adaptation of the Stephen King novel *The Dead Zone*. The filmmaker chose the site because of its dark reputation.

The tunnel dates back to the mid-1800s, when workers were building the Grand Trunk Railway through the Niagara area. The land around was wet, and fields were prone to flooding, so the railway was built on a raised mound. The workers constructed an arched limestone tunnel, about forty metres long, running under the track from one side to the other. That way, water draining from the fields could flow under the track without washing the earth away.

During dry periods, local farmers used the tunnel as a convenient shortcut. The tunnel was wide enough to walk or ride through, and although the path might be muddy, it was an easier route than climbing up the bank, crossing the track, and then descending the other side.

People still cut through that tunnel, but today they are wary. The tunnel is said to be haunted and has been named the Screaming Tunnel because of the terrifying ghost who lingers there.

Various stories speculate about the ghost's origins. Here is one version we have heard.

There used to be a group of houses not far from the south side of the tunnel—a small community that never grew into a town and is now long gone. If you search among the trees nearby, the foundations of the buildings can still be found. An older couple lived in a farmhouse here. They had no children of their own, but when a relative died, leaving an orphaned daughter, they did the Christian thing and took the child into their own house. They found themselves in the role of caregivers.

From the start, it was an unhappy pairing. The couple were religious, strict, and rigid in their ways, while the girl was solitary and strange. She didn't like her new guardians, and for some reason they seem to have been uneasy around their new ward. Something about her didn't seem quite right. Sometimes she was seen wandering in the fields or along the track, apparently talking to herself. At other times, she went into the tunnel, scratching odd markings into the limestone bricks.

The girl's odd behaviour drew the attention of neighbours, which embarrassed the couple, but although they chastised the girl, and even beat her, she still kept up her strange ways, and tensions grew between the girl and her guardians.

One night, the girl left her bedroom. In the kitchen, she found a box of matches. Hunched over them with fascination, she struck one match after another, lighting scraps of paper, the kerosene lamp, the lace

curtains . . . Soon the whole kitchen was alight. If the girl had intended revenge against the old couple, she was successful—the fire quickly engulfed the house, and her guardians died. But the girl was also caught in the inferno. By the time she escaped the house, her hair and clothes were ablaze. It's said she ran to the tunnel, screaming as she burned, and died at that spot. Her ghost still haunts the tunnel.

There are many other variants of the story. Some say the girl was the daughter of the couple and the fire was an accident. Others say the girl was a murder victim, and her killer burned her body. But most versions describe a girl burning and dying in the tunnel.

Most commentators also agree on how to summon the ghost—or how to provoke it. Those who want to come face to face with the ghost of the Screaming Tunnel must go into the tunnel late at night (midnight is best) with a box of old-fashioned wooden matches. You'll need a flashlight as you pass through the stone arch at the entrance to the tunnel. It's a damp place. The ground is often wet and covered with stones.

Make your way to the middle of the tunnel. Then, if you dare, turn out the flashlight and wait in the darkness. Some people say they can feel the presence of the ghost around them. If you do, light a wooden match. As the match flares, you will hear the ghost give a bloodcurdling scream, and then a pair of unseen lips will blow the match out.

One more thing. Although the ghost is most famously heard, some people have reported seeing a ghostly figure—the silhouette of a girl—standing against the dim light of the entrance. According to some accounts, she beckons the visitor to come to her, as if she wants to show them something. But don't go. Because they say that what she will show you, as you draw closer, is the remains of her face.

SURVIVAL DOS AND DON'TS

If you venture into the wilderness, aways take a knife,
so you can divide up your last Tic Tac.

What do you do if you're lost in the wilderness? People have used some interesting strategies to cope and survive.

One of the most challenging situations is being out in bad winter conditions. Keeping warm becomes an absolute priority. Two teens from British Columbia proved that.

According to a report on CBC News, the friends had gone snowboarding near Nelson, at Whitewater Resort, which is famous for its powder snow. They entered an out-of-bounds area, and as the snow fell more and more thickly, they were unable to find their way back.

The police began a search for the missing kids that night, but as the weather grew worse, they had to suspend their work. The next day, the weather was still bad, but the clouds lifted just enough to send out a helicopter.

The helicopter scoured the area near the resort. Searchers were afraid they might return with two bodies, but they found the kids alive and well.

The teens knew rescuers would arrive eventually and that it was important to stay in one place, so they had built a shelter in the snow and started a fire to keep themselves warm and act as a signal. That's not easy to do in a snowstorm, but one of the pair had used the school homework in his backpack to help keep the fire going.

People were impressed by the survival skills of the snowboarders. "They did all the right things," said one official.

But you have to wonder—if they were going to take a trip into the out-of-bounds area to go snowboarding, why did they take a backpack full of homework? This wouldn't just be an excuse to get an extension on their school assignment, would it? "Honest, I finished my essay on time, but I had to burn it so I could survive!"

* * *

The following January, CBC News reported on another BC teen out lost in the snow. He had been snowmobiling with a group near the town of 100 Mile House, in central British Columbia. The seventeen-year-old became separated from the rest of the party and ended up at the bottom of a steep slope. The others didn't notice he was no longer with them at first, and he couldn't find a way out.

When his party realized he was missing, they criss-crossed the area looking for him, but could find no sign of the teen. They called for help from search and rescue, who set to work. At 10:30 that night, they finally found him.

In the six hours he'd been lost, the teen had put his snowmobile out in the open, so it could be easily seen by searchers, then went into a wooded area where he built himself what they described as "an incredible snow cave." Despite having made a good start on his winter palace, the teen was described as being very relieved when a search party showed up. According to a rescue team leader, "He couldn't stop thanking us enough."

* * *

Sometimes, people are stuck in the wilderness for longer periods. They solve the problem of shelter, but then they need to think about food. In such cases, staying alive may depend on careful rationing—

although some people take this to extremes.

One camping couple went for a hike near the village of Keremeos, in British Columbia's southern interior. They didn't come back. Search crews went out but were unable to find the couple. After a week, there was still no sign of them, and family members braced themselves for the worst.

It turned out that the hikers had become lost near the base of a mountain. They had no equipment, no way to start a fire, and no way to signal, but they were able to build a shelter. The only food they had with them consisted of snacks—two oranges, three cookies, nine Tic Tacs, and two Werther's Originals.

They carefully rationed their food supplies and moved from place to place, trying to find their way back (an unwise move, according to rescue experts).

Fortunately for them, they did eventually manage to find a route back to civilization. After seven days, the couple walked into a lodge, a little dehydrated but alive. They had clearly been fastidious about rationing, but it was a close call. Of their original candy-based food supply, they had eaten two oranges, three cookies, eight Tic Tacs, and two Werther's Originals. All that remained was one Tic Tac.

There's a lesson here. If you venture into the wilderness, aways take a knife, so you can divide up your last Tic Tac.

Another important survival tip is making sure you have a way to call for help. You can't rely on getting a phone signal on your mobile. On the other hand, if you do get a phone signal, it makes sense to use it. Unfortunately, it seems not everyone got the memo.

On an October morning in 2021, an American hiker (CTV News reports didn't reveal the person's name, age, or sex) left to explore the trails around Mount Elbert, the highest peak in the Rocky Mountains. The hiker hadn't returned by evening, and a search operation began.

The hiker had a mobile phone, but repeated calls to the number went unanswered. Was the hiker incapacitated? Had they fallen? Searchers checked areas where they figured hikers were likely to shelter or to have gotten into trouble. They kept searching far into the night, but there was no sign of their lost hiker.

The next day, the searchers received good news. After twenty-four hours in the wilderness, it seemed the hiker had found the trail, made it back to their car, and checked back in at the place they were staying.

Officials from the rescue service talked to the hiker to confirm they were okay. The officials were a little puzzled that they hadn't been able to get through on the phone.

"Oh, that." The hiker explained they had declined all those calls.

The officials were astonished. Why, when a person is lost in the mountains, would they decline multiple phone calls from searchers?

The hiker, who seemed to be more worried about nuisance calls than survival, replied, "I didn't recognize the number."

THE PHANTOM LIGHTHOUSE KEEPER

*Sometimes he goes into the lighthouse,
and an eerie light appears where the lamp used to be.*

Just south of the bustling streets of Toronto is Centre Island, which, together with several smaller islands, curls into Lake Ontario, making a natural harbour around the city's waterfront. On the southernmost tip of Centre Island, at the end of a winding path through bushes and trees, is a lighthouse, a hexagonal stone tower more than two centuries old, gazing out across the lake.

Although the lighthouse lies only a few kilometres from the city, you wouldn't know it if you stood there. It feels quiet and remote, surrounded by greenery. Some find it peaceful, but others say *forlorn* would be a better word. It is a lonely place.

Visitors tell of strange events here. When the mist rolls in from the lake, some have heard moans in the distance. Others report seeing a light shining from the lighthouse beacon, although the structure is locked up and nobody is there to operate it. People who have been allowed to inspect the interior of the lighthouse have commented on the disturbing sense that they have invisible company, and say they heard footsteps moving on the stairs.

And there are reports of grisly sightings—a mutilated figure, a man, walking around among the trees and bushes, searching in vain for . . . something.

But who is this figure? And what is he searching for?

Locals say the phantom is the ghost of the original lighthouse keeper, who died a violent death at the lighthouse and now haunts the area.

In life, his name was Paul Radelmüller, and he had lived a varied and interesting life. He came from the same part of Bavaria as the British royal family, and as a young man, he had been a servant to Prince William Henry, brother of King George III. Later, he moved to Canada and worked as a steward for the lieutenant-governor of Nova Scotia. Around 1804, he moved to the Toronto area, hoping to start a German-language school.

It was a tense time to live in "muddy York." The United States was looking to expand and eyeing the colony to the north. The British set up their defences, preparing for an attack on Canada from across the lake. They built a stronghold on what are now the Toronto Islands. In those days, they weren't islands—the land was a peninsula curling around from the mainland. It was a perfect place to harbour ships and looked like a good defensive position—so good, in fact, that the southern tip was named Gibraltar Point, after Britain's impregnable island fortress in the Mediterranean.

The stone lighthouse was an important part of Toronto's defences. Although it looks a modest tower today, only about five storeys high, it was once the tallest building in the region, and it was the first stone building in the Toronto area. Back then, most houses were constructed from wood, and even nearby Fort York was made of logs. The lighthouse could warn friendly ships away from the jutting land with its lamp or by sounding a horn, while the keeper could keep an eye on ship movements. If American ships were to attack, the keeper was well placed to warn the soldiers at a nearby blockhouse. This small fort stood on guard with a single powerful cannon facing out towards the lake, ready to blast red-hot incendiary cannonballs at any attacking ships.

The position of lighthouse keeper was an important one, and in 1808, trusty Paul Radelmüller got the job. He lived in a nearby cabin with his wife and young daughter. For years, he lit the whale-oil lamp at night, tending the lamp and keeping watch on ship movements.

But his life wasn't all work. The keeper enjoyed beer and always kept a keg handy. By some accounts, he brewed it himself. According to a later keeper, Radelmüller was well known as a friendly host. Soldiers from the blockhouse would visit him in the evening, and he'd invite them in to sit and drink beer with him. For seven years, he continued in the job. But his hospitality would lead to his death.

One night in 1815, as the war with America was coming to its close, two British soldiers arrived at Radelmüller's door, ready to enjoy a few beers with the lighthouse keeper. They had already been drinking heavily, and Radelmüller soon decided he'd had enough of their boisterous company. They demanded beer. The lighthouse keeper refused. The soldiers became argumentative, then violent . . .

The next day, Radelmüller was gone. He had mysteriously disappeared. If it's true, there must have been obvious signs of violence, because the *York Gazette* reported that "from circumstances, there is every moral proof of his having been murdered." The two soldiers who visited him were imprisoned, but when they were put on trial for the killing, there seems to have been insufficient evidence to convict them.

Eighty years later, another lighthouse keeper became interested in the story. He had heard that Radelmüller's body had never been recovered. He explored the area and found a human jawbone. It supported a local story that the soldiers had killed their host, then chopped up his body, burying it in several nearby locations.

Radelmüller's spirit did not rest peacefully. It's said that he still wanders. Sometimes he goes into the lighthouse, and an eerie light appears where the lamp used to be. But at other times, his ghost restlessly searches the grounds. And perhaps the story explains what he has been doing for the past two hundred years— he's hunting for the rest of his dismembered corpse.

ALCHEMISTS OF THE NIGHT

*How do these little insects produce so much
light without generating any heat?*

On a hot summer evening, just after sunset, you can see the lights of the fireflies as they perform their aerial dance to find a mate. In large numbers, they may even synchronize their lights, producing a spectacular display.

People are often surprised when they set eyes on the creature that produces these pyrotechnics. Many imagine the insect as something fairy-like, pale and delicate, perhaps with gossamer wings and a long, flowing tail.

The reality seems slightly disappointing at first. The firefly is not a fly at all. It is just a little beetle with a long, slender body. The front of the body is red and black. Behind are two sleek wing covers, brown or black with a crisp yellow outline. There is no hint of the fairy here. It looks more like an insect business executive, smartly dressed for a meeting.

But the firefly's appearance changes when it launches itself into flight. The black wing covers snap forward, transparent wings extend, and the beetle's abdomen hangs down, displaying its signature light coming from the segments near the tip.

One common species in Canada is the big dipper firefly. The name comes from its flying pattern. The insects fly up and down as if they're on a fairground ride, turning their yellow-green lights on and off as they follow a J-shaped flight pattern a couple of metres above the ground. But the name fits in another way too—in the Northern Hemisphere, the little insects perform their dance when the Big Dipper is most prominent in the sky. Only the males perform this flying display. There will often be many males, competing for a single female. She sits somewhere nearby, on a branch or a piece of tall grass. She watches the male display and occasionally responds with an encouraging return flash. "Keep it up, boys. I'm still deciding."

Scientists have long been fascinated

by the glow of the firefly—particularly by how efficient the lighting is. How do these little insects produce so much light without generating any heat? And how are they able to turn their lights on and off so rapidly and so precisely, without the residual glow you'd see from a luminous clock?

The firefly's light comes from a chemical called luciferin. When air is pumped into the chambers holding luciferin and several other chemicals, a bright light is produced. Another chemical signal can instantly turn the light off again. When the air supply is cut off, the light goes out. The colour varies by species. Some fireflies produce yellow light, while others glow orange or green.

The firefly light has been used in medicine. Researchers in England placed firefly genes inside cancer cells. This caused the cells to glow, making them susceptible to light-activated chemicals. Similar techniques can also be used to identify the presence of cancer—the bad cells literally light up. Scientists are now finding ways of doing the same chemical trick without needing to extract chemicals from thousands of fireflies.

Firefly adults don't live long—only a couple of months. But the brevity of their lives is deceptive. As with many insects, what we call their adulthood is more like extreme old age. They have taken their adult form to find a mate and produce the next generation, going out in a blaze of light.

Which raises the question, What were they like before they became adults?

Have you seen *Star Trek II: The Wrath of Khan*? If you have, you'll surely remember the "ear bug" scene, where the villainous Khan takes a gruesome, snapping, segmented creature from its tank and places it in Chekov's helmet. It crawls across his face, enters his ear, and burrows through to his brain, controlling his mind. It was the stuff of nightmares.

The larva of the firefly looks very like that creature. It is much smaller—and has absolutely no interest in human ears (or any other part of us)—but if you happen to be a snail, or a slug, or an earthworm, it is as much a monster as its science fiction lookalike. If a hunting firefly larva comes across the trail of a snail or slug, it follows it, crawling along and stalking the mollusk. Once it catches up, it seizes its unfortunate prey and injects it with poison before eating it alive.

Other firefly larvae live in water. They are particularly fond of feasting on mosquito larvae, which helps keep mosquitoes under control. If insects can be divided into friend and foe, the fireflies are definitely "on our side."

The larvae are also commonly known as glow-worms. They don't shine brightly like the adults, but if they're disturbed by an enemy, they will give off a soft glow, warning any predator that they are not good to eat. That's because fireflies don't just produce chemicals that glow or digest prey. They can also produce chemicals that kill a predator.

Their best weapon is called lucibufagin. It is similar to the poisons produced by toads, and it makes the firefly taste extremely unpleasant to the spiders and birds that might otherwise eat them. Most will instantly spit out the firefly. Those that don't will usually be killed by the poison. Both the hunting larva and the glittering adult are protected by this toxic substance. This might seem like an excellent defence—and usually it is—but the same chemical can also be the downfall for the little beetles.

There is a type of firefly called Photuris that covets the protective elixir. Photuris glows just like other fireflies, but it is unable to produce the same poison, making it a potential victim for predators. But Photuris has evolved a devious way of getting the precious substance. When the big dipper fireflies are performing their mating flights, it finds a branch and sends out signals that resemble those of the female big dipper. As the males approach, it seizes them and eats them. Not only is it immune to their protective chemicals, it can absorb those chemicals and use them for its own protection. This insect is nicknamed "the femme fatale firefly."

So when the evenings are warm, turn out the porch lights and watch the aerial ballet of the fireflies. These alchemists of the night have spent their short lifetimes removing slugs and snails from our gardens and mosquitoes from our ponds. Now, in their final weeks of life, they dance in the air, desperately competing to impress a female and produce the next generation. It's a final flight of spectacular beauty, and for each shining participant it will end in romantic success, empty disappointment, or sometimes cruel betrayal.

DIFFERENT STROKES

The sky was mostly clear, with just one big cloud.
Suddenly he was hit by lightning.

It's an amazing thing to watch lightning flash over a forest or lake. But if you're out in that storm, the experience can be terrifying. After all, what if you get hit?

Lightning can hurt a person in various ways. The deadliest event is the direct strike—a single bolt of lightning hitting a person. Fortunately, this is very rare.

We're often told not to get close to a tree during a thunderstorm. One reason is that lightning might hit the tree and send a branch down on top of you. Another is the danger of a "side flash." That's when lightning hits a tree but jumps sideways on its way down to the ground and continues its journey using the nearest person's body. Victims are usually people trying to take cover from the rain accompanying the storm.

A third way lightning can hurt you is through ground current. That's where lightning hits an object, then travels out along the ground. On its way, it may go through a person's body, going up one leg and down the other. If the legs are far apart, this can be fatal. Occasionally, newspapers report herds of cows all killed by one lightning strike. Their legs are widely spaced, and it's the ground current that kills them, not a giant strike from above. If you're caught in a storm, crouching low and keeping your feet together will give some protection against ground current.

People often say that golfers are most likely to be hit by lightning. The statistics say otherwise. You are more likely to be struck while playing soccer than playing golf, while running is a close third for risk. But by far the most dangerous activities are on or near water. Of course, fishing and boating are dangerous, and so is swimming, but just sitting or standing on a beach is also a high-risk activity.

Luckily, the odds of being struck by lightning at all are low. In fact, when people quote long odds, they often use the lightning rod as their yardstick.

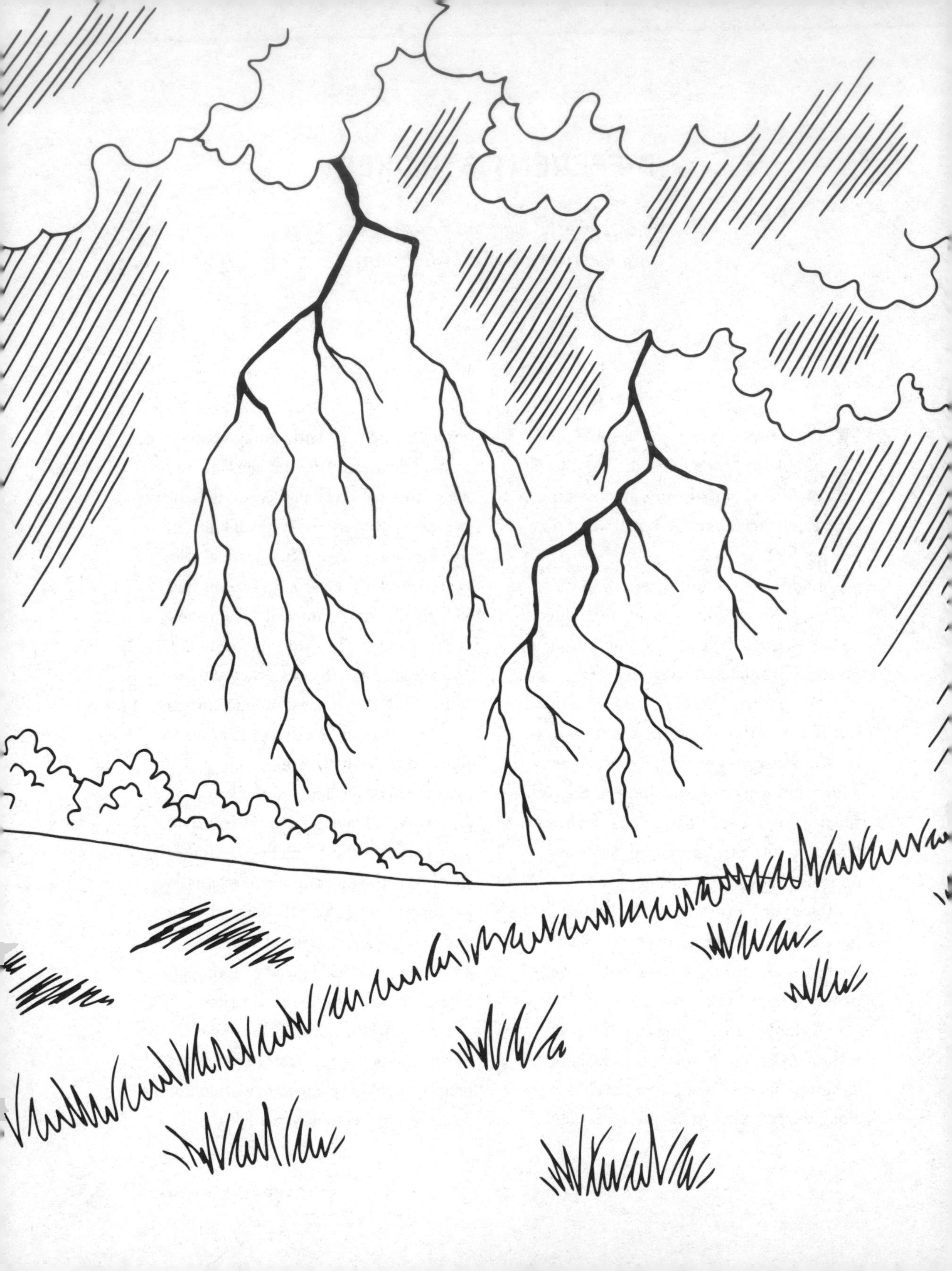

It's said you're more likely to be struck by lightning than you are to win the lottery. One Canadian did both. At the age of fourteen, he was putting a boat away by a lake. (That increases the odds a bit.) As he tells it, the sky was mostly clear, with just one big cloud. Suddenly he was hit by lightning.

In 2015, when he was an adult, he won Atlantic Lottery's Lotto 6/49, walking away with a 50 percent share of a million-dollar win. The other half went to his co-worker. According to mathematicians, the odds of these two events happening to one person are one in trillions.

* * *

The comedy group the Frantics used to have a running feature about a superhero named Mr. Canoehead. In the sketch, he is portaging through Algonquin Park when a lightning strike welds his aluminum canoe to his head, transforming him into "Canada's greatest aluminum-headed crimefighter."

But sometimes life imitates art. In 1994, the *Canadian Journal of Plastic Surgery* described a case of a man who was out in his motorboat when a storm blew up. He was struck by lightning, and it welded his hand to the steering wheel. In his case, however, the hand was part of a prosthetic arm, and it was possible to remove him from the boat by taking off the arm. He received a few burns from the incident but made a complete recovery.

* * *

Because boats are closer to the sky than their surroundings, they are often targets for lightning.

In 2020, a Labrador family was out on their boat. The weather can change fast in that part of the country. They saw the skies darkening and lightning flashes getting closer, so they quickly turned for shore.

One of the boat's occupants was in the habit of holding onto the boat's metal canopy poles, but on this occasion, she thought she should keep her hands away from them. It was a smart move. As the boat sped through the water, a big lightning bolt hit the vessel. The passengers heard a colossal bang—it sounded as if a bomb had gone off.

The lightning had struck the boat's metal antenna, blowing it apart. The surge of electricity destroyed almost all the electronics on board. The engine was dead and smoking. The radio was out. The two navigation systems were out. Even the windscreen wipers were burnt out.

One passenger was hurt—she was bleeding from over her eye. It turned out that a sharp fragment from the exploding

antenna had lodged in her forehead.

Fortunately, the family had a satellite phone with them, and it was one of the few pieces of electronics to survive the strike. They called for help and got safely back to shore, where the injured passenger was treated.

The boat was repaired too, at a cost of more than $25,000. But the family wasn't complaining. The boat was carrying hundreds of litres of fuel—it might easily have gone up in a fireball. They felt lucky to be alive.

* * *

Scientists who have studied lightning strikes say the bolt often enters through the wettest parts of the head—the eyes, ears, mouth, and nose. The electricity often converges at the base of the brain, which controls the heart and breathing.

If a person's heart stops, it will often restart on its own—the heart can beat even when it is separated from the brain. Breathing is different. If the brain is stunned, breathing stops, and the unconscious victim silently suffocates.

So if you are around someone who is struck by lightning, give them mouth-to-mouth resuscitation (no, there won't be any lingering electrical charge on them), and don't give up. It can take quite a while for the brain to recover from the shock.

Many people who appear dead will eventually start breathing on their own and go on to make a full recovery.

* * *

Lightning likes to make its way to grounded electrical equipment, so using that gear outdoors in stormy conditions can be a risk.

In 2017, CTV News reported on a man who was giving a speech at an outdoor wedding in an orchard at Woodstock, New Brunswick. The clouds had started rolling in, but the reception continued as planned. The father of the bride was giving his speech, but just as he was getting to the part about what a lucky man his new son-in-law was, everyone heard a loud bang as the speaker was struck by lightning.

The man was shocked, in every sense, and onlookers were horrified. He was holding a microphone in his hand, and the mic and his arm were all lit up, making him look like Zeus wielding a thunderbolt.

Amazingly, the bride's father wasn't hurt at all by the strike, although he said he felt the electricity run through him. After it happened, he wasn't quite sure what to do next, so, being a cool customer, he kept going with his speech. Frantic helpers intervened, taking back the micro-phone and hurrying him to a nearby tent. Others joined them as the skies opened and rain came down in sheets.

Nobody could believe that being struck by lightning had not injured the man, but the only damage was a little scorch mark on his thumb. He even joked that, after being struck, his sore knee felt a little better.

We like his attitude. That's the thing about lightning. If you get hit, you just have to know how to conduct yourself.

"I THINK IT'S ABOUT SNACKS O'CLOCK."

—Hangry Camper

Good Eats

INTRODUCTION

FOR MORE AND MORE OF US, NOTHING BEATS GETTING BACK TO BASICS, LIKE COOKING ON A BARBECUE, A FIRE PIT, OR A CAMPFIRE. FOOD TASTES SO MUCH BETTER WHEN IT'S COOKED *EN PLEIN AIR* AND EATEN *AL FRESCO* IN THE GLOW OF THE SETTING SUN.

When you're at the cottage, the last thing you want to do is to spend hours cooking, but basking in the great outdoors gives you an appetite for healthy, filling food. In the following pages, you'll find a selection of quick and easy recipes that take the hard work out of cottage and campfire cooking so you can throw together a tasty meal with minimal fuss.

The key to success is to use the best-quality ingredients you can find, and to cook them in the simplest ways. Most of our delicious recipes feature just a few ingredients, keeping in mind smaller pantries and spaces and simpler living at the cottage. And let's be honest, prepping is quicker when there's less food to chop and grate.

It's said that food is good for the soul—and so are a few nights eating under the stars. Not only does everything taste so much better when it's cooked over a grill or an open fire, but there are fewer dishes to do! If you want to get back to nature and enjoy a simpler life, all you need is the right gear, a sense of adventure, and these handy go-to recipes.

GETTING STARTED

Cooking outdoors isn't complicated, but there are some things you should know that will make it safer and more enjoyable. Here's some useful information, guide lines, and tips to get you started.

COOKING ON A CAMPFIRE

1. Ensure that the area around your fire is clear of debris and well away from any overhanging trees, bushes, or wooden fences. Have safety equipment (a hose, sand bucket, or fire extinguisher) close at hand. Ideally, you should light your fire at least an hour before you plan to cook, to ensure it is hot enough.

2. Collect some dry twigs to use as kindling. Place them in the centre of your fire pit, along with some crumpled-up newspaper and tinder (smaller bits of kindling). Cover with some more twigs and use matches to start a fire. (To speed up this process, you can cheat and use some lump charcoal in place of the initial kindling.)

3. When the kindling is burning, place some larger logs on top (kiln-dried logs will generally light faster than air-dried logs). Keep a stack of logs close by for adding to the fire as the evening goes on.

4. Wait for the flames to die down before you start cooking. If you're planning on ember roasting, you may find it helpful to scrape some hot embers out of the main fire and create a designated and accessible cooking area near the edge. Level them out to fit the size of your pan. When the wood has burnt down to glowing embers, which are grey and ashy, you can place a cast-iron pot or skillet directly on top of them. Or you can add corn on the cob or baking potatoes, wrapped in a double layer of aluminum foil.

5. If the embers are still glowing red, however, raise the pan above the fire— about 4 inches (10 cm)—on a trivet or grill grate, supported on bricks, or suspend it from a camping tripod.

COOKING ON A FIRE PIT

Many people are turning to portable fire pits as an alternative to traditional wood fires. A fire pit is safer, easier to control, and provides heat and light as well as being a great place to gather and cook. Unless you have a portable propane fire pit, the best fuels to use are kiln-dried logs or lump charcoal. Most fire pits come with a grill grate or rack that fits on top for grilling over the fire. Or you can place a cast-iron pan or skillet directly on the grate. For stews, soups, and casseroles, you can hang a large heavy-bottomed pot from a camping tripod above the fire.

COOKING ON A CHARCOAL BARBECUE

You can cook on a portable charcoal barbecue in the same way as you would at home, following the steps below. Set it up well away from any overhanging trees, bushes, or wooden fences. For the best results, use sustainably produced hardwood lump charcoal, which is free from fire accelerants—it is not only environmentally friendly, but it will also smell nicer and won't affect the taste of the food.

1. Stack the lump charcoal in the barbecue with some scrunched-up newspaper and a few twigs.

2. Light the newspaper and wait for the charcoal to catch fire and for the flames to die down before cooking over the glowing ashen embers. If there are still flames, wait a little longer.

3. For cooking steaks, chops, burgers, and vegetables directly over a high heat, spread out the coals evenly in a single layer. If the coals are glowing white but still a little red in the middle, they are really hot and perfect for direct cooking these types of foods.

4. For cooking food slowly (e.g., fish fillets and bone-in chicken) or keeping it warm after it has been fully cooked, push some coals away from one side of the barbecue and place the food on the rack above this area, while more food is cooking directly above the heat on the other side. Or if the coals are very hot but ashen white, you can cook food more slowly above them or place foil parcels within them.

TIPS FOR COOKING OUTDOORS

Cooking in the great outdoors is not like preparing meals in your kitchen at home. But with a little organization, careful planning, and the right equipment, you can still eat like royalty.

1. Keep it simple—now is not the time to be adventurous or experimental.

2. Prep ahead and get everyone involved —give friends and family jobs to do.

3. Limit the number of ingredients you cook with—it will make storage easier and cooking much simpler.

4. Plan your meals and keep all the utensils you'll need handy.

5. When using pots and pans outdoors, cook with the lids on to keep out any dust or bugs.

6. Pre-measure and prep ingredients— e.g., grated cheese, nuts and seeds, spice mixes, and vinaigrettes—in resealable bags or containers.

7. Plan breakfast the night before.

GOOD EATS

CHILI CITRUS MARINADE

This marinade is so easy to make and tastes great on grilled chicken, shrimp, and even mushrooms. Don't like crushed red pepper? Use some dried or chopped mint, thyme, or rosemary instead. Or add a clove of crushed garlic or a generous pinch of garlic powder.

MAKES A GENEROUS ¼ CUP (75 ML)
PREP 5 MINUTES

3 TBSP (45 ML) OLIVE OIL
JUICE OF 1 SMALL LEMON
A GOOD PINCH OF CRUSHED RED PEPPER

Combine all of the ingredients in a resealable bag or container, seal, and shake well. Add the food to be marinated. Seal and gently turn or shake to coat. Refrigerate for 1 hour before cooking over the fire.

HONEY MUSTARD MARINADE

Use this marinade for vegetables and tofu as well as steaks and chicken. To make this vegan, substitute pure maple syrup or agave syrup for the honey. You can also add some chopped fresh herbs, such as basil or thyme, if desired.

MAKES A GENEROUS ⅓ CUP (90 ML)
PREP 5 MINUTES

3 TBSP (45 ML) GRAINY MUSTARD
2 TBSP (30 ML) OLIVE OIL
1 TBSP (15 ML) LIQUID HONEY
1 TSP (5 ML) WHITE WINE VINEGAR
JUICE OF 1 SMALL LEMON

Combine all of the ingredients in a resealable bag or container, seal, and shake well. Add the food to be marinated. Seal and gently turn or shake to coat. Refrigerate for at least 1 hour before cooking over the fire.

QUICK & EASY BARBECUE SAUCE

*You can make this sauce in advance or you can rustle it up in less
than 10 minutes using just a few pantry ingredients.*

MAKES A GENEROUS 1½ CUPS (ABOUT 400 ML)
PREP 5 MINUTES | COOK 5 MINUTES

1¼ CUPS (310 ML) TOMATO
KETCHUP

2 TBSP (30 ML) WORCESTER-
SHIRE SAUCE

1 TBSP (15 ML) SOY SAUCE

1 TBSP (15 ML) RED WINE
VINEGAR

1 TBSP (15 ML) DIJON OR
GRAINY MUSTARD

JUICE OF ½ LEMON

2 TO 3 TBSP (30 TO 45 ML)
LIGHT BROWN SUGAR

½ TSP (2.5 ML) GARLIC POWDER

½ TSP (2.5 ML) CHILI POWDER
OR SMOKED PAPRIKA

1. In a saucepan, combine the ketchup, Worcestershire,
soy sauce, vinegar, mustard, lemon juice, sugar, garlic
powder, and chili powder.

2. Place the pan over medium heat. Once the sauce
starts to bubble gently, simmer, stirring occasionally,
for 4 to 5 minutes.

VARIATIONS
- You can use liquid honey instead of brown sugar.
- For a more intense tomato flavour, add 2 tbsp
  (30 mL) tomato paste.
- If you don't have a fresh lemon, use 2 tbsp (30 mL)
  bottled concentrated lemon juice (or to taste).
- Add some heat with a few drops of Tabasco or
  Sriracha sauce.

TIPS
- This sauce makes a wonderful marinade for chicken
  and spare ribs (just cool before using).
- Serve as a dip for grilled vegetables, shrimp, and
  chicken.

GOOD EATS

GUACAMOLE

Freshly made guacamole tastes so much better than ready-made alternatives found in supermarkets. Enjoy as a dip for tortilla chips, potato chips, or crunchy vegetables. Or serve with tacos, burritos, or fajitas or plain grilled chicken, shrimp, or vegetables. It's so versatile.

SERVES 4 | PREP 10 MINUTES

1 HOT GREEN OR RED CHILI (E.G., SCOTCH BONNET PEPPER), SEEDED AND DICED

½ SMALL RED ONION, DICED

2 GARLIC CLOVES

½ TSP (2.5 ML) COARSE SEA SALT

2 OR 3 RIPE AVOCADOS

JUICE OF 1 LIME

A SMALL BUNCH OF CILANTRO, LEAVES AND STEMS, CHOPPED

1 RIPE TOMATO, SEEDED AND DICED

FRESHLY GROUND BLACK PEPPER

1. Using a pestle and mortar, crush together the chili, red onion, garlic, and salt until well combined. Set aside.

2. Cut the avocados in half and discard the pits. Using a spoon, scoop out the flesh and place it in a bowl. Using a fork, roughly mash the avocado (don't overdo it—you want to keep it slightly chunky). Stir in the lime juice.

3. Add the chopped cilantro, reserved chili mixture, and diced tomato. Gently stir everything together, just until combined. Season with black pepper, to taste.

VARIATIONS
- Use scallions instead of red onion.
- Crushed red pepper or bottled chilies can replace a diced fresh chili but won't taste quite so good.

TIP
Guacamole will keep for 2 to 3 hours before the avocado starts to discolour.

LATE SUMMER CORN RELISH

The contrasting colours, flavours, and textures make for a spectacular relish. If you can find one, use a local melon. This recipe makes a lot of relish, but it can be easily halved. And it goes well with grilled chicken, grilled fish, or a bowl of tortilla chips—and even works as a stand-alone salad.

MAKES ABOUT 8 CUPS (2 L)

6 CUPS (1.5 L) FINELY DICED
WATERMELON

4 EARS COOKED CORN
(GRILLED OR BOILED),
KERNELS REMOVED (ABOUT
3 CUPS/750 ML)

1 CUP (250 ML) MINCED RED
ONION

1 JALAPEÑO PEPPER, SEEDED
AND FINELY DICED

½ CUP (125 ML) FRESH
CILANTRO LEAVES, ROUGHLY
CHOPPED

1 TBSP (15 ML) GROUND CUMIN

JUICE OF 2 LIMES

TABLE SALT

In a bowl, carefully combine the watermelon, cooked corn, onion, jalapeño, cilantro, cumin, and lime juice (you want the watermelon to retain its shape). Season with salt, to taste. Taste and adjust seasonings, as desired. Refrigerate for at least 1 hour before serving. Best when served fresh.

PIZZA

Nothing tastes better than a wood-smoked or chargrilled pizza. We've cheated here and made ours with pitas, naans, or flatbreads instead of the usual dough base. These make an easy light meal when you're in the great outdoors, especially if you eliminate chopping by using canned and bottled toppings.

SERVES 4 | PREP 15 MINUTES | COOK 7 TO 12 MINUTES

4 LARGE PITA BREADS, NAAN
   BREADS, OR FLATBREADS
OLIVE OR VEGETABLE OIL, FOR
   BRUSHING
8 TBSP (120 ML) PASSATA OR
   BOTTLED NAPOLETANA OR
   PIZZA SAUCE
3½ OZ (100 G) BOTTLED ROASTED
   RED PEPPER STRIPS
7 OZ (200 G) MUSHROOMS,
   SLICED
5 OZ (150 G) FRESH MOZZARELLA,
   PACKED IN BRINE, SLICED
SEA SALT AND FRESHLY GROUND
   BLACK PEPPER

1. Light a campfire at least 1 hour before you are ready to cook, or preheat your barbecue. When the campfire flames have died down and the ash is grey, or the barbecue is really hot, lightly brush one side of the pitas, naans, or flatbreads with oil and place, oiled-side down, on the barbecue grill or a lightly oiled rack or grill grate set over the fire.

2. Once the pizza bases are lightly browned underneath, transfer them to a tray and brush the top (ungrilled) sides with oil.

3. Flip the bases over so the grilled side is facing up. Spread the passata or sauce evenly over each base, right up to the edges. Then scatter the peppers and mushrooms over top and cover with the sliced mozzarella. Season with salt and pepper, to taste.

4. Carefully place the pizzas back on the grill. Loosely tent each with aluminum foil or cover with the lid of the barbecue. Cook for 5 to 10 minutes, until the cheese has melted and is golden brown and bubbly. Serve immediately.

VARIATIONS

- Make it your way: top with shredded cooked chicken or ham, pepperoni, sliced cooked sausages, cooked bacon, pineapple, thinly sliced zucchini or eggplant, cherry tomatoes—your imagination is the limit.
- If you don't have fresh vegetables on hand, use canned or bottled artichoke hearts, corn niblets, or mushrooms.

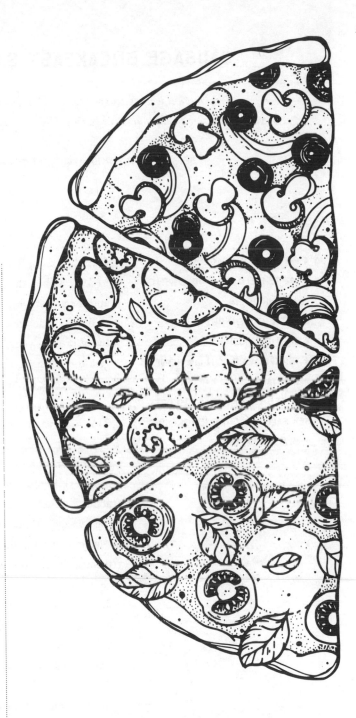

GOOD EATS

SAUSAGE BREAKFAST SANDWICHES

Breakfast outdoors tastes even better when you eat it with your hands.
If you're planning to move along or go for a hike, this is the perfect on-the-go sandwich.

SERVES 4 | PREP 10 MINUTES | COOK 20 MINUTES

4 FAT PORK SAUSAGES

4 LARGE FIELD OR PORTOBELLO
MUSHROOMS

A LITTLE OIL OR BUTTER

4 ENGLISH MUFFINS

4 TSP (20 ML) DIJON OR HONEY
MUSTARD

4 SLICES OF CHEDDAR CHEESE

SEA SALT AND FRESHLY GROUND
BLACK PEPPER

1. Light a campfire at least 1 hour before you are ready to cook. When the campfire flames have died down and the ash is grey, grill the sausages in a cast-iron skillet on a rack over the glowing embers. Alternatively, preheat your barbecue and, once it is really hot, grill the sausages in a skillet over the hot coals. You can also cook the sausages over a stove top.

2. Whichever cooking method you use, cook the sausages, turning occasionally, until cooked through (no longer pink inside) and browned all over (about 10 minutes). Before the sausages are fully cooked (after about 5 minutes) add the mushrooms to the pan with the sausages. If needed, drizzle the mushrooms with a little oil or dot with butter, and cook for 5 minutes, turning once, until tender and golden brown.

3. Meanwhile, split the English muffins and lightly toast them on the grill. Spread a little mustard on 4 halves of the toasted muffins. Top each one with a grilled sausage, cut in half, and a grilled mushroom. Season with salt and pepper and top with a slice of cheese. Cover with the remaining toasted muffin halves.

4. Wrap each breakfast sandwich in a square of aluminum foil, twisting the ends to seal it. Place the foil packages on the grill or over the fire for 4 to 5 minutes or until the cheese melts. Eat immediately.

VARIATIONS
- For a veggie breakfast sandwich, grill vegetarian sausages or thick slices of halloumi or tofu.
- Add a fried egg or a slice of beefsteak tomato to each sandwich.

TIPS
- Serve with tomato ketchup or hot sauce.
- For extra flavour, combine crushed garlic and/or herbs with a couple tablespoons of olive oil, and then slather all over the mushrooms before cooking them.

SPEEDY BEEF & BLACK BEAN CHILI

Make this delicious chili in a cast-iron Dutch oven placed over a fire or on a barbecue or on a simple stove top. A Dutch oven is such a useful pot when you're cooking outdoors because heat can be applied to the food from above (if you place hot coals on the lid) as well as below. And because cast iron holds heat so well, your food cooks more evenly. It's the perfect one-pan solution.

SERVES 4 | PREP 10 MINUTES | COOK 1¼ HOURS

2 TBSP (30 ML) OLIVE OIL OR
   VEGETABLE OIL
1 LARGE ONION, CHOPPED
3 GARLIC CLOVES, CRUSHED
1 RED BELL PEPPER, SEEDED
   AND DICED
2 TSP (10 ML) HOT CHILI POWDER
½ TSP (2.5 ML) CAYENNE PEPPER
1 LB 2 OZ (510 G) GROUND BEEF
2 X 14-OZ (398 ML) CANS
   CHOPPED TOMATOES
2 TBSP (30 ML) TOMATO PASTE
1 X 14-OZ (398 ML) CAN BLACK
   BEANS, RINSED AND DRAINED
1 CUP (250 ML) BEEF BROTH
SEA SALT AND FRESHLY GROUND
   BLACK PEPPER
1 CUP (100 G) COARSELY GRATED
   CHEDDAR CHEESE
TORTILLA CHIPS, FLATBREADS,
   OR CRUSTY BREAD, TO SERVE

1. Light a campfire at least 1 hour before you are ready to cook, or preheat your barbecue. If you're cooking this over a campfire, let it burn down to the embers and place a grill grate over them. Alternatively, cook on a stove top.

2. Heat the oil in a cast-iron Dutch oven over a medium heat. Add the onion, garlic, and red pepper and cook, stirring occasionally, for 8 to 10 minutes, until the vegetables have softened. Stir in the chili powder and cayenne pepper, and cook for 1 minute.

3. Add the ground beef and cook, breaking it up with the back of a spoon, for 5 to 10 minutes, until the meat is browned all over.

4. Stir in the tomatoes, tomato paste, beans, and broth. Cover the pot and simmer the chili for 30 minutes. Remove the lid and cook, uncovered, for another 30 minutes, or until the liquid has reduced to a fragrant, spicy sauce. Season to taste with salt and pepper.

5. Ladle into bowls and sprinkle with the grated cheese. Serve with some tortilla chips, warmed flatbreads or pitas, or crusty bread for dipping.

VARIATION

For a vegetarian chili, omit the ground beef, increase the quantity of onions and peppers to taste, and add an extra can of beans.

TIPS

- If you're cooking this over a fire, try to keep the heat even (add more logs or charcoal, if necessary).
- For a very spicy chili, use canned or bottled jalapeños.
- You can use red kidney beans instead of black beans.
- If you don't have fresh garlic, substitute $1/8$ tsp (0.5 mL) garlic powder.

GOOD EATS

LENTIL SLOPPY JOES

Sloppy Joes are great camping food: they're easy to make, don't require any special ingredients, cook in one pot, and—best of all—you can eat them using your hands. This version, made with lentils, is perfect for vegans and vegetarians, but they're so tasty that meat lovers will enjoy them, too.

SERVES 4 | PREP 10 MINUTES | COOK 35 MINUTES

2 TBSP (30 ML) OLIVE OIL OR VEGETABLE OIL

1 MEDIUM YELLOW ONION, FINELY CHOPPED

3 GARLIC CLOVES, CRUSHED

1/3 CUP (80 ML) TOMATO PASTE

7 OZ (200 ML) JARRED TOMATO SAUCE

1 CUP (250 ML) DRIED RED LENTILS

1½ CUPS (375 ML) VEGETABLE BROTH

1 TO 2 TBSP (15 TO 30 ML) COCONUT SUGAR
   OR PURE MAPLE SYRUP

1 TSP (5 ML) APPLE CIDER VINEGAR

1 TSP (5 ML) DIJON MUSTARD

1 TBSP (15 ML) VEGAN WORCESTERSHIRE
   SAUCE

1 TSP (5 ML) CHILI POWDER

SEA SALT AND FRESHLY GROUND BLACK
   PEPPER

4 LARGE BURGER BUNS

SLICED RED ONION, TOMATOES, AND
   LETTUCE, TO SERVE (OPTIONAL)

1. Light a campfire at least 1 hour before you are ready to cook, or preheat your barbecue. If you're cooking this over a campfire, let it burn down to the embers. Alternatively, cook on a stove top.

2. Heat the oil in a cast-iron Dutch oven over a medium heat. Add the onion and garlic, and cook for 6 to 8 minutes, until softened.

3. Stir in the tomato paste and tomato sauce, and then add the lentils and broth. Cover and cook for 15 minutes or until the lentils are tender but not mushy and most of the liquid has been absorbed.

4. Stir in the coconut sugar or maple syrup (to taste), vinegar, mustard, Worcestershire sauce, and chili powder. Cook for 10 minutes or until the lentil mixture is thick. Season with salt and pepper, to taste.

5. Split and toast the burger buns. Top half of the toasted buns with the lentil mixture. Garnish with onion, tomato, and lettuce (if using). Cover with the remaining buns and serve immediately.

TIPS

- Spice these up with some ground cumin or smoked paprika.
- Add some diced red or green (bell) pepper.
- If you like spicy food, add more chili powder or drizzle with hot sauce.

GOOD EATS

ONE-POT MAC 'N' CHEESE

You will need a Dutch oven or a heavy cast-iron saucepan with a lid to cook this fan favourite, prepared over an open fire, as heat is applied from the top as well as the bottom. This allows the pasta to steam inside the pot, as in a conventional oven, resulting in the perfect melty cheese dish.

SERVES 4 | PREP 5 MINUTES | COOK 10 TO 15 MINUTES

3 CUPS (300 G) DRIED
  MACARONI PASTA

2 CUPS (500 ML) WHOLE MILK

1 CUP (250 ML) WATER

2 TBSP (30 ML) SALTED BUTTER

1 CUP (250 ML) EVAPORATED MILK

3 CUPS (300 G) GRATED CHEESE
  (E.G., SWISS, CHEDDAR,
  PARMESAN)

1 TBSP (15 ML) DIJON MUSTARD

A GOOD PINCH OF GARLIC
  POWDER

SEA SALT AND FRESHLY GROUND
  BLACK PEPPER

CAYENNE OR CHILI POWDER,
  FOR DUSTING

1. Light a campfire at least 1 hour before you are ready to cook. Let it burn down to the embers and place a grill grate over them.

2. In a large Dutch oven, combine the macaroni, whole milk, water, butter, and a good pinch of salt. Cover with the lid.

3. Place the pot on the grill and then carefully put some glowing hot coals on the lid. Cook for about 10 minutes, or until the macaroni is just tender but retains some bite (al dente), and there's still a little cooking liquid in the pot.

4. Stir in the evaporated milk, cheese, mustard, and garlic powder (if possible, use a tripod or grill with legs to raise the Dutch oven higher above the embers). Cook, stirring continuously, until the cheese melts and the sauce coats the pasta.

5. Season to taste with salt and pepper. Serve immediately, dusted lightly with cayenne or chili powder.

VARIATIONS

- Stir in some handfuls of baby spinach leaves, sliced scallions, halved cherry tomatoes, or a diced jalapeño pepper at the end of Step 4, and heat until the spinach has wilted and the tomatoes are warmed through.
- Add some diced ham or crispy bacon bits at the end of Step 4, and heat until warmed through.
- For a different flavour profile, use a mixture of crumbled blue cheese and grated cheese.
- For a crunchy topping, sprinkle with crushed cheesy crackers, potato chips, or tortilla chips just before serving.

TIP

Garnish with chopped fresh parsley or chives.

GOOD EATS

ALL-IN-ONE BARBECUED FAJITAS

This is an easy way to cook fajitas on the barbecue—using foil means there's less mess and nothing falls through the bars. This is also a very versatile dish: you can add almost anything you like to the foil packages. For a flavour boost, dust the chicken and vegetables with some fajita seasoning before cooking (available from most supermarkets and delis).

SERVES 4 | PREP 15 MINUTES | COOK 10 TO 15 MINUTES

OLIVE OIL, FOR BRUSHING AND DRIZZLING

4 BONELESS, SKINLESS CHICKEN BREASTS, CUT INTO STRIPS

1 RED BELL PEPPER, SEEDED AND CUT INTO STRIPS

1 GREEN BELL PEPPER, SEEDED AND CUT INTO STRIPS

1 YELLOW BELL PEPPER, SEEDED AND CUT INTO STRIPS

2 ONIONS (WHITE OR RED), THINLY SLICED

1 TO 2 CHILI PEPPERS, SEEDED AND DICED

8 LARGE CORN OR FLOUR TORTILLAS

A HANDFUL OF FRESH CILANTRO (LEAVES AND STEMS), CHOPPED

SEA SALT AND FRESHLY GROUND BLACK PEPPER

SALSA, PICO DE GALLO, GUACAMOLE (PAGE 38), SOUR CREAM, HOT SAUCE, AND LIME WEDGES, TO SERVE

1. Heat your barbecue on the medium to medium-high setting, or until the flames die down and it's hot.

2. Meanwhile, lightly brush four 12- x 12-inch (30 x 30 cm) squares of aluminum foil with oil. Divide the chicken, peppers, onions, and chilies evenly among them. Season with salt and pepper, to taste, and drizzle with olive oil. Bring the sides of each square of foil up into the centre and twist them together to make a sealed package.

3. When the barbecue is hot, carefully place the sealed packages on the grill and, if you have one, cover with the lid (don't worry if you don't have one; the chicken might just take a little longer to cook). Cook for 10 to 15 minutes, until the chicken is cooked through (reads 160°F/325°C on a meat thermometer and is no longer pink inside) and the vegetables are tender.

4. Carefully open the foil packages and sprinkle with the chopped cilantro. Set aside, keeping warm.

5. Warm the tortillas on the barbecue for 1 to 2 minutes per side.

6. To serve, give everyone their own foil package and tortillas so they can assemble their fajitas: Divide the chicken and vegetables among the tortillas and top with pico de gallo, guacamole, sour cream, a drizzle of hot sauce, and a squeeze of lime. Roll up or fold over the filled tortillas and eat with your hands.

TIP

You can also cook the foil packages in the glowing hot coals of a campfire for 15 to 20 minutes.

MEXICAN-STYLE GRILLED CORN

This recipe is inspired by a popular Mexican street food: grilled corn slathered in chili butter and sprinkled with crumbled Cotija cheese. This version omits the cheese, but if you want to try it, crumbled feta makes a good substitute.

SERVES 4 | PREP 10 MINUTES | COOK 10 TO 15 MINUTES

4 LARGE EARS OF CORN, HUSKS
   REMOVED
OLIVE OR VEGETABLE OIL, FOR
   BRUSHING
SEA SALT AND FRESHLY GROUND
   BLACK PEPPER

CHILI LIME BUTTER
¼ CUP (60 ML) SALTED BUTTER,
   SOFTENED
1 HOT RED CHILI PEPPER,
   SEEDED AND DICED
1 GARLIC CLOVE, CRUSHED
GRATED ZEST AND JUICE OF
   1 LIME
A HANDFUL OF FRESH CILANTRO
   (LEAVES AND STEMS), FINELY
   CHOPPED

1. Heat your barbecue on the medium to medium-high setting, or until the flames die down and it's hot.

2. Make the chili lime butter: in a bowl, combine the butter, chili, garlic, lime zest and juice, and cilantro.

3. Lightly oil the grill of the hot barbecue and place the corn on top. Cook, turning frequently, for 10 to 15 minutes, until the corn is tender, starting to char, and is golden brown all over.

4. Serve the hot corn topped with the chili lime butter.

VARIATIONS
- If you don't have a fresh chili, you can substitute 1 tsp (5 mL) chili powder or ground chipotle pepper. Alternatively, serve the corn with Sriracha or sweet chili sauce.
- Substitute ¾ tsp (3 mL) crushed red pepper for the fresh chili.
- To make a dip instead, substitute an equal amount of mayonnaise for the butter.

ROASTING CORN OVER A FIRE

CORN COOKS TO SMOKY PERFECTION OVER THE
HOT EMBERS OF A CAMPFIRE. THE TRICK IS TO
COOK IT IN THE HUSKS–THEY'RE A GOOD NATURAL
COVERING, PROTECTING THE JUICY NIBLETS FROM
DRYING OUT. SOAK THE CORN COBS IN COLD WATER
FOR 30 MINUTES BEFORE COOKING TO SOFTEN
THE HUSKS. THEN PAT THE CORN DRY, PEEL BACK
THE HUSKS–LEAVING THEM ATTACHED TO THE BASE
OF THE CORN–AND CAREFULLY DISCARD THE SILKY
THREADS INSIDE. REPLACE THE HUSKS, COVERING
THE CORN, AND THEN COOK FOR 20 TO 30 MINUTES
ON A GRATE OVER THE EMBERS, JUST UNTIL THE
CORN IS TENDER. ALTERNATIVELY, WRAP SOME
HUSKED CORN COBS IN ALUMINUM FOIL AND PLACE
ON THE HOT GRATE.

GARLICKY CAMPFIRE POTATOES

Everyone loves potatoes, and the good news is that they are so easy to cook over a fire or on a barbecue. Just wrap the potatoes in foil and forget about them for half an hour. These garlicky spuds go great with grilled steak, chicken, chops, and fish.

SERVES 4 | PREP 10 MINUTES | COOK 30 TO 40 MINUTES

2 LB (1 KG) SMALL NEW POTATOES

¼ CUP (60 ML) OLIVE OIL, DIVIDED

4 TO 6 GARLIC CLOVES, CRUSHED, DIVIDED

A GOOD PINCH OF CRUSHED RED PEPPER

1 TSP (5 ML) CHOPPED FRESH ROSEMARY, THYME, OR OREGANO LEAVES, DIVIDED

SEA SALT AND FRESHLY GROUND BLACK PEPPER

1. Light a campfire at least 1 hour before you are ready to cook, or preheat your barbecue. If you're cooking this over a campfire, let it burn down to the embers and place a grill grate over them.

2. Take four large squares of aluminum foil and divide the potatoes evenly among them. Lift the edges of the foil up around the potatoes towards the centre to create a bowl, and then drizzle each package of potatoes with an equal amount of oil. Divide the garlic, crushed red pepper, and herbs evenly among them. Season each with a good grinding of salt and pepper.

3. Seal the foil packages by twisting the edges of the foil together and crimping them between your fingers (the idea is to enclose the potatoes securely but loosely).

4. Place the packages on the barbecue grill or a grate set just above the hot coals and cook for 30 to 40 minutes, moving the packages around occasionally, until the potatoes are tender.

VARIATIONS

- For a brighter flavour, add some grated lemon zest and a squeeze of lemon juice.
- If you don't have fresh garlic on hand, use $^1/_8$ tsp (0.5 mL) garlic powder.
- For cheesy garlicky potatoes, add some grated Parmesan cheese.
- Try adding some capers, anchovy fillets, or chopped scallions, to taste.

TIP

If you don't have fresh herbs, you can use dried herbs without compromising flavour (as a general rule, use one-third the amount of fresh herb called for).

CAUTION!

Be careful when opening the hot foil packages. They will be full of hot steam. It's a good idea to pierce the foil before opening to release the steam.

MORE S'MORES!
SHAKING UP THE CAMPFIRE CLASSIC

IT'S HARD TO BEAT THE COMBINATION OF GRAHAM CRACKER, TOASTED MARSHMALLOW, AND CHOCOLATE, BUT IF YOU'RE FEELING ADVENTUROUS, HERE ARE SIX MORE WAYS TO ENJOY A COTTAGE TRADITION.

POTATO CHIP S'MORE
SUBSTITUTE THICK RUFFLED POTATO CHIPS FOR GRAHAM CRACKERS AND ENJOY A SWEET AND SALTY TREAT.

ELVIS S'MORE
SPREAD PEANUT BUTTER ON A GRAHAM CRACKER. ADD BACON, BANANA, AND TOASTED MARSHMALLOW.

S'MOREOS
REMOVE (OR EAT!) THE WHITE FILLING OF AN OREO AND SUBSTITUTE A TOASTED MARSHMALLOW. OR SIMPLY ADD AN OREO TO THE MIDDLE OF YOUR S'MORE. OR, GO WILD AND PUT YOUR MARSHMALLOW BETWEEN TWO OREO COOKIES.

BREAKFAST S'MORE
START YOUR DAY WITH MELTED CHOCOLATE AND A TOASTED MARSHMALLOW BETWEEN TWO MINI PANCAKES.

NUTELLA S'MORE
SLATHER CHOCOLATE HAZELNUT SPREAD ON THE GRAHAM CRACKERS AND ADD A TOASTED MARSHMALLOW.

REESE'S PEANUT BUTTER S'MORE
SWAP OUT THE CHOCOLATE FOR A REESE'S PEANUT BUTTER CUP.

JULY 1 STRAWBERRY SUPREME

Celebrate Canada Day and local strawberries
with this decadent and boozy dessert.

SERVES 8

1 CUP (250 ML) HEAVY (WHIP-
    PING) CREAM
1 PINT (500 ML) VANILLA
    ICE CREAM
JUICE OF 1 LEMON
¼ CUP (60 ML) COINTREAU OR
    GRAND MARNIER LIQUEUR
    (OPTIONAL)
8 CUPS (2 L) FRESH STRAW-
    BERRIES (WHOLE IF SMALL,
    HALVED IF LARGER), HULLED

1. Using a whisk or electric mixer, whip the cream until soft peaks form. Set aside.

2. Place the ice cream in a large bowl and, using a wooden spoon, gently beat until just softened.

3. Fold the whipped cream, lemon juice, and Cointreau or Grand Marnier (if using) into the softened ice cream.

4. Add the strawberries and stir gently, just until combined. Serve immediately.

BLUEBERRY SEASON'S BEST MUFFINS

Blueberries and honey are a marriage made in heaven. This recipe calls for an oven, so you can make these muffins at the cottage or in advance and bring them with you. Pick up some local berries and honey and fill your kitchen with the aroma of summertime.

MAKES 12 MUFFINS

BUTTER OR OIL, TO GREASE
   THE PAN
1½ CUPS (375 ML) ALL-PURPOSE
   FLOUR
1 TSP (5 ML) BAKING POWDER
½ TSP (2.5 ML) BAKING SODA
¼ TSP (1 ML) TABLE SALT
1/3 CUP (80 ML) LIQUID HONEY
¼ CUP (60 ML) UNSALTED BUTTER
1/3 CUP (80 ML) WHOLE MILK
½ TSP (2.5 ML) FRESHLY GRATED
   LEMON ZEST
2 TBSP (30 ML) FRESH LEMON
   JUICE
1 LARGE EGG
1½ CUPS (375 ML) FRESH
   BLUEBERRIES

1. Preheat the oven to 350°F (180°C). Line the wells of a 12-cup muffin pan with cupcake liners or grease with oil or melted butter. Set aside.

2. In a large bowl, sift together the flour, baking powder, baking soda, and salt. Make a well in the centre of the dry ingredients. Set aside.

3. In a small saucepan, combine the honey and butter, and gently heat until the butter has melted (alternatively, heat in a microwave in a small bowl). Stir until well combined. Set aside to cool.

4. In another small bowl, beat together the cooled honey mixture, milk, lemon zest and juice, and egg. Add this wet mixture to the well of the dry ingredients and, using a wooden spoon, gently stir just until combined (be careful not to overmix).

5. Gradually fold in the blueberries, being careful not to crush them too much.

6. Using a spoon, fill each muffin cup about two-thirds full.

7. Place the pan in the preheated oven and bake for 30 to 35 minutes, until a toothpick inserted in the middle of a muffin comes out clean.

8. Remove the pan from the oven and let the muffins cool in the pan for about 5 minutes before transferring to a wire rack to cool completely.

"DID I EVER TELL YOU ABOUT THE TIME . . . ?"

—Rested and Reminiscing

Campfire Stories

THE POOR PAWPAW

Custard apple, hadi'ot, sweetsop, soursop, dog banana, Quaker delight, wild banana, cherimoya, umbi, ylang-ylang, and banango.

You can find some nice snacks in the wilderness, if you know your plants and berries. Indigenous Canadian fruits include cranberries, saskatoon berries, and blueberries, not to mention squash and pumpkins. But there's one Canadian fruit that rarely gets talked about—the pawpaw.

It gets a brief mention in Disney's version of *The Jungle Book*, where the friendly bear Baloo sings to Mowgli about the "bare necessities"—advising him how to eat fruits like the pawpaw. The bear must have had his pawpaws imported, because there are no pawpaws in Mowgli's South Asian jungle home—they are an American fruit.

The range of the pawpaw tree covers the eastern United States and as far north as Southern Ontario, meaning the pawpaw is one of Canada's largest indigenous fruits, and the largest really sweet one. Sure, pumpkins and squash are larger, and a botanist will tell you they are

technically fruits, but in the kitchen they tend to be thrown into the "veg" category. No hungry kid ever sank their teeth into a ripe pumpkin.

The pawpaw is a strange outlier—a tropical fruit growing in a temperate climate. The little tree that produces it looks like it belongs in a rainforest, with its drooping, dark green leaves. Its ripe fruit resembles a smallish green mango. You can test it with a squeeze. If it feels like a ripe peach, you can cut it open to reveal a bounty of delicious soft, yellow fruit, with a row of large, shiny seeds in its centre.

Remove the seeds and squeeze the skin to push out the edible flesh. It has the consistency of soft ice cream or custard and is very sweet. The taste—people struggle to describe it—is like a combination of other, more familiar fruits: mango and banana are often mentioned (which is where one of the fruit's names, banango, comes from). Some are reminded of pear and pineapple.

Pawpaws grew in North America long before humans arrived. It's thought that the plant evolved to coexist with giant herbivores that once roamed the Americas—mammoths, mastodons, and giant ground sloths. The huge creatures ate the fruit whole, then spread the seeds around, along with a dollop of fertilizer, as they wandered from place to place. These creatures were driven to extinction after humans arrived on the continent, but somehow the pawpaw has kept going—perhaps because prehistoric humans liked the fruit and deliberately scattered the seeds.

The tree is related to the magnolia and produces a dark purple flower with three big petals, looking a little like a trillium. It has a yeasty odour—not pleasant to humans but intoxicating to the beetles and flies that pollinate the tree. Some scientists think the plant's smell is attractive to the kinds of insects that are drawn to carrion. Old-time farmers certainly believed this—they would try to improve their pawpaw patches by hanging roadkill on the tree branches.

Most plants protect themselves from insects and browsing animals using natural chemicals, and the pawpaw is no exception, producing powerful toxins in its leaves and branches—although not in the yellow fruit flesh. The pawpaw is a sturdy tree, resistant to most insects and plant diseases. But some insects thrive on its poisons. If you happen to see a

zebra swallowtail butterfly flitting by, there's probably a pawpaw tree nearby too, because this butterfly grew up eating pawpaw leaves and rarely strays far from its favourite plant. The striped black-and-white butterfly, and its handsome striped caterpillar, are completely immune to the pawpaw tree's defences. The caterpillar feasts on the leaves, allowing the plant's toxins to accumulate in the insect's body. The second-hand poisons are an effective protection. A predator that makes the mistake of eating one of these butterflies will not eat a second.

Pawpaws can be found in the wild, and unlike some wild fruits, they're not too difficult to cultivate. The delectable fruit was once an important part of North American cuisine, both for the Indigenous Peoples and for settlers. That probably accounts for the confusing array of names it has been given—custard apple, hadi'ot, sweetsop, soursop, dog banana, Quaker delight, wild banana, cherimoya, umbi, ylang-ylang, and banango. Even the name *pawpaw* is confusing—it's a corruption of *papaya*, which grows in the Caribbean and is an unrelated fruit.

Pawpaws used to be very popular in the Americas. George Washington was said to be a fan, and Lewis and Clark ate them on their expeditions. The fruit was often eaten raw, added to pancakes, or baked into desserts. Geographic features were named for the prized fruit. There are at least seven Paw Paw Lakes in the United States and eleven communities named Paw Paw.

But pawpaws suddenly went out of fashion in the twentieth century. During the Great Depression, many Americans couldn't afford bananas, so they ate pawpaws instead. The fruit acquired some new nicknames—"hillbilly mango" and "the poor man's banana." The stigma of being associated with poverty affected its popularity.

There's another reason you won't usually find pawpaws in the average grocery store today. The delicate pawpaw bruises easily, and its shelf life is only a few days. Researchers in Kansas have been working on this problem and are trying to develop new variants that will produce a longer-lasting, supermarket-friendly fruit. Someday, they may appear on the shelves.

Until then, if you want to try a pawpaw, you'll probably need to wait until you stumble on them at a farmer's market—and they won't be cheap.

Or, if you're lucky, you may be able to follow the zebra swallowtails and get your fruit straight from the tree.

CAMPFIRE STORIES

INTO THE FLAMES

"I didn't even think of the dangers. . . . I just did what I had to do."
—CLARK WHITECALF

Clark Whitecalf knows a thing or two about fire. As a young man trying to find his way in the world after a stint in residential school, he left his home on Saskatchewan's Sweetgrass Reserve and relocated to Saskatoon. He took odd jobs to pay the bills, including work with the mop-up crew of a forest firefighting unit. Dropped onto scorched earth in the far reaches of northern Saskatchewan, he'd pick his way carefully through the debris, putting out spot fires wherever they threatened to flare up.

By the time August 31, 2015, rolled around, a now forty-year-old Whitecalf was back in Sweetgrass, married to Samantha Moccasin, and father to five children. Life was good. Set in the rolling grasslands just west of North Battleford, the Cree reserve was a beautiful place to raise a family. Clark worked construction, although a broken leg that hadn't completely healed had slowed him down a bit. That night, his newly licensed sixteen-

year-old daughter, Masey, asked if she could practise her driving skills. At about 9:30 p.m., they all piled into the truck and hit the road—Masey, Clark, and Samantha squeezed into the front and fifteen-year-old Hailey sat in the back. They hadn't been out for long when Masey spotted a faint orange glow up ahead. Not taking her eyes off the road, she said, "I think Sonya's house is on fire."

Clark and Samantha knew the family that lived there: Sonya and Joe Fineday and their teenaged children. What they didn't know was whether anyone was home. Clark switched seats with Masey and drove quickly, arriving to find the bungalow engulfed in flames—and a truck parked in the driveway. By the time the volunteer firefighters arrived, it would be too late to save anyone. They had to act now.

Clark and Samantha pounded at the locked front door, but it brought no response. Clark felt his sense of unease increase. If someone was inside, it was possible they'd been injured or overcome by smoke. Maybe they weren't able to call out for help. Forgetting all about his still-healing leg, he kicked in the door, but a black cloud of smoke stopped him in his tracks.

Leaving Samantha and Masey calling into the house through the open front door, and Hailey on the phone with emergency services, Clark ran to the side entrance. He got into the house this time and made it as far as the kitchen before the smoke and the flames pushed him out again.

Back in front of the house, he was met by Samantha and his two daughters, both of whom were crying. Samantha told him that an orange cat had come out of the front door and started pacing on the lawn and meowing. They'd taken the animal's distress as a sign that someone was still inside, and she and Masey had crawled through the front door on their stomachs, taking care to stay beneath the billowing smoke. This time, when they'd called out, they heard a noise.

"Clark," Samantha said, "there's somebody inside."

He didn't hesitate. Once again he approached the front door. As his wife and daughter had done, he stayed close to floor, pulling himself through the smoke on his stomach. Off and on, he could hear a girl's voice, though he couldn't tell where it was coming from. He peered through the smoke and the flames into the living room, where he saw an arm hanging over the edge of the couch. It belonged to a young woman. Jolei Farness, the Finedays' eighteen-year-old daughter.

It took Clark three tries to get her out the front door.

Once outside, working with Samantha, Clark rolled Jolei onto her side. After a tense moment or two, during which Samantha was sure the young woman wasn't breathing, Jolei started to cough. As Clark made one last trip into the house to check for anyone he might have missed, Samantha and the girls heeded Clark's warning to get away from the burning house—and the large propane tank sitting in the yard. Gently, they helped Jolei to stand and walk to her uncle's house, just across the road. Clark stayed behind, moving whatever he could out of the path of the flames, until the volunteer firefighters arrived.

As the paramedics took Clark to a local hospital, where he was treated for severe smoke inhalation, Jolei was transported two hours southeast to Saskatoon. The next day, the young woman struggled to put the pieces of the evening together. She remembered coming home, looking at Facebook on her iPad, and then nothing until she woke up at the house across the street from her own, screaming as Samantha poured cold water on her burns. Now, suffering from smoke inhalation, a hole in her lung, and second- and third-degree burns, she listened as a nurse told her how close she'd come to dying.

"They said if I'd been in there for one or two minutes more, I wouldn't be alive," she recalls.

Three months later, she was out of the hospital and visiting a relative when Clark Whitecalf happened to stop by. At first, he didn't recognize her. She said hello, showed him the burn scars, and gave him a hug. For Clark, that's when the enormity of the situation began to sink in. "I'm starting to realize if we didn't drive by that night, she wouldn't be alive," he recalls.

The meeting left him feeling awkward, he says, "But I also felt really good."

Clark was honoured for his bravery in 2016. In October, the couple travelled to Regina, where Lieutenant-Governor Vaughn Solomon Schofield presented Clark with a Royal Canadian Humane Association Silver Medal for Bravery. That December he was awarded a Carnegie Medal in recognition of the extraordinary risk he took in rescuing Jolei.

"The situation inside the building was a deadly situation," said Eric Zahren, executive director of the Carnegie Hero Fund Commission, "potentially deadly for even a very short exposure, and his exposure was not short."

More accolades followed. In 2017, Clark received a Queen's Certificate for Bravery and the Gold Stanhope Medal, awarded only once a year for the entire Commonwealth.

Clark is proud of the awards and humbled. His memories of everything that happened that night are still a bit hazy, but he remembers the thought that was running through his head. "I thought there's a person that's going to die if no one [does] anything about it, so I guess God picked me to go and save her, I don't know," he says. He's not sure if it was his old firefighting instincts or something else, but from the moment he saw the flames, he knew he was going to try to help. "I didn't even think of the dangers," he says. "I just reacted. I just did what I had to do."

And because he did, a young woman is alive and well.

THE LADY OF ALBION FALLS

Some have seen her silhouette on moonlit nights. And when the air is quiet and still, they say you can still hear her distant cries.

When the land cracked to form the Niagara Escarpment, it created the world-famous Niagara Falls. But this is not the only waterfall to tumble over that precipice. Other streams and rivers flow over the escarpment, creating other waterfalls.

One of these is Albion Falls, located not far from Hamilton. Oak, ash, and maple trees cling for dear life to the steep slopes, and running between them, Red Hill Creek flows over the escarpment, forming a steep cascade of frothing white water tumbling over the dolostone and shale rocks. At nineteen metres in height, the waterfall is beautiful, but high enough to be deadly.

It's said that, long ago, a woman named Jane Riley lived in the area. She was in love with a local man, Joseph Rousseau. They came from very different family backgrounds. The Rousseaus were affluent, while Jane's family was an ordi-

nary farming family with an Irish background—at a time when there was often prejudice against the Irish. Conscious of these problems, Joseph kept the relationship secret for a while, but the more he saw of Jane, the more charmed he was by her. They went on romantic walks and picnics together, through the local woods and countryside. One of their favourite spots was Albion Falls. It was at that romantic spot that he finally asked Jane for her hand in marriage. Jane said yes.

But their happiness did not last long.

Joseph told his mother about the engagement. Mrs. Rousseau was a strong-willed and controlling woman. When she learned that her son had proposed to this young woman, without her permission, she was furious. An Irish girl from a poor family? This Jane was obviously a greedy gold digger chasing after her son for the money. No, this match was entirely unacceptable. She would not allow her son's life to be ruined by his youthful folly.

Joseph begged and pleaded with his mother, insisting she had misread the situation. He tried to explain how much he loved Jane. He spoke of how sweet and kind his fiancée was, and how hardworking and decent her family. He assured his mother that, over time, she would come to love Jane as much as he did. But the more he spoke, the more opposed his mother became to the match. She was alarmed and threatened by the depth of her son's love for Jane Riley, and she vowed she would disown her son if he married her. Mrs. Rousseau knew how to manipulate Joseph, and she pressured him so much, and made his life such a misery, that the young man finally weakened, and against his better judgment, he agreed to do what his mother asked.

Joseph met with Jane. He explained the situation and told her he needed to break off the engagement. They must never see each other again.

He returned to his mother's house. But if Mrs. Rousseau thought the breakup would end her problems, she was wrong. Her son regretted his action and resented his mother's part in it. He missed Jane. Without the woman he loved, he became sullen and miserable.

Joseph may have been sad about ending the relationship, but Jane was devastated. She was completely unable to cope with this cruel rejection. She stopped eating. She barely slept. She wandered,

alone and forlorn, through the woods where she and her lover used to walk. Those who saw her said she looked lost and dishevelled. People said she would get over it, but time brought no healing. Her heartbreak was too much to bear. At last, she went to the cliffs near the waterfall and jumped, falling to her death.

The community was shocked by the tragedy. Some knew about the mother's interference and spoke disapprovingly about what she had done.

Joseph's mother was also shocked. She hadn't anticipated that her actions would lead to a death. And she now realized— much too late—that the love between Jane and her son was real. For his part, Joseph could not forgive his mother, and he cursed himself for listening to her. The mother worried that she had poisoned her relationship with her son.

Mrs. Rousseau had another worry too. Call it superstition or a presentiment, but she became convinced that Jane's ghost was looking for revenge against her. Jane may have been a kind figure in life, but the mother believed that, after death, Jane's vindictive ghost was coming for her, travelling back from the falls, through the trees, looking to punish Mrs. Rousseau for destroying her chance at happiness.

People reported seeing a figure in the woods—it looked just like Jane, but the figure disappeared as they approached. Others reported hearing cries in the night—sometimes heartbroken sobs, and sometimes the echoes of Jane's final scream.

Mrs. Rousseau also heard these strange sounds and felt a mounting sense of dread. She told people she was sorry for what she'd done, that it was a mistake and she'd accepted the blame for Jane's death. But her repentance didn't improve her relationship with her son, and it didn't settle her own nerves. She couldn't shake the growing feeling that his dead fiancée had unfinished business with her and was coming to settle the score.

The fateful moment came at a social gathering. Mrs. Rousseau seemed particularly uneasy that evening. She saw movements out of the corner of her eye and heard sounds behind her that others could not hear. She tried to distract herself by talking to a neighbour. An uncomfortable feeling was growing inside her, but she tried to hide it, becoming more animated, almost manic. In the middle of the conversation she suddenly gasped. When the neighbour asked her what was wrong, she said, with horror, that she could feel Jane's hand on her shoulder. The neighbour saw nothing. A moment later, Mrs. Rousseau dropped to the ground, dead.

Jane Riley had taken her revenge.

It is said the young woman's ghost still haunts the area around the top of the falls. Some have seen her silhouette on moonlit nights. And when the air is quiet and still, they say you can still hear her distant cries.

In daytime, Albion Falls is a beautiful spot for a romantic walk or picnic. But if your romance goes well, and you feel the urge to get engaged at that particular location, make sure you keep your promise—or you may feel Jane's hand on your own shoulder.

SO LONG, SUCKERS!

At Toronto's Pearson Airport, a trained sniffer beagle picked up an interesting smell from one passenger's luggage.

Canada's border control agents often catch criminals trying to smuggle exotic animals into the country. The creatures are usually reptiles, like tortoises and snakes, but in May 2019, they stopped a man smuggling something a little more unusual.

At Toronto's Pearson Airport, *National Geographic* reported that a trained sniffer beagle picked up an interesting smell from one passenger's luggage and drew the attention of officers to it. When they looked inside a grocery bag the man had kept with his carry-on luggage, they found five thousand squirming, live leeches.

The owner of the bag, "Sergey," had flown in from Russia. He claimed he was going to use the leeches himself, pouring their wastewater on his orchids. It didn't sound plausible.

Government naturalists identified the type of leech as *Hirudo medicinalis*—also known as European medical leeches.

These are voracious parasitic worms, distant relatives of the earthworm, that love to latch onto humans and suck their blood. They are called medical leeches because the same species has been used since ancient times in medicine. People once believed that removing surplus blood could cure disease, and leeches are enthusiastic about removing your surplus blood—which, in the leech's tiny mind, is as much of it as it can eat. In the 1800s, demand for the wriggling horrors reached such a high level that wild leeches became endangered, leading to strict rules on their international trade.

Medical use of leeches today is very limited—their anticoagulant saliva can occasionally be useful in keeping blood vessels open after certain surgical procedures, but that's about all. However, there is a steady demand for them in the "quack medicine" market.

The medical leeches bred for use on humans are raised in clean conditions. An analysis of Sergey's collection showed that they were leeches taken from the wild, and that they had been dining on whatever they could find in their stagnant ponds or dirty streams. A New Ager using one of these to "cleanse bad blood" might end up with a serious infection.

A single medical leech can sell for $10, meaning that Sergey's haul was worth up to $50,000. It didn't seem likely he'd bought them for his flowers. Officials guessed he was intending to sell them to gullible alternative-medicine customers. The leeches were confiscated, and Sergey was charged for trying to import a protected species. After a guilty plea, he was banned from importing any more live animals and given a $15,000 fine.

Case closed. Bag emptied.

Except for the pesky question of what to do with the five thousand leeches.

The creatures posed a real problem for the officials. They didn't want the fuss and expense of looking after such a large number of bloodsuckers. The leeches were lively, and good escape artists. Twenty escaped after a water change and had to be recaptured. The leeches weren't native to Canada, so it would be an ecological problem to release them into the wild.

Furthermore, while most of us might look at a leech and think, "Kill it! Kill it with fire!" the fact is that they are a threatened species. So, in the end, the leeches were spared a fiery death and patiently cared for at taxpayers' expense while officials tried to find a place for them. It took a few months, but eventually the leeches were safely passed on to interested researchers at various museums and academic institutions.

The final tally: five thousand bloodsuckers were relocated and confined for the rest of their lives, and one was released after paying a large fine.

S'MORES

For years, chocolate *only meant a high-end drink.*

Among the most popular of all campfire snacks are s'mores, those gooey sandwiches of golden roasted marshmallow and chocolate between two pieces of graham cracker. Some people like to wrap the assembled package in foil and give it a final roasting. Whatever way you make it, the final snack is as delicious as it is hot and messy.

Of course, the name is a contraction. After you've had the first one, you'll say, "I want s'more!" The recipe goes back at least to the 1920s, when it was popular with Boy Scouts and Girl Scouts, but the three ingredients are much older and have three very different origins.

First, the marshmallow. Long before the familiar fluffy candy puffed up in popularity, *marsh mallow* meant a plant, a herb with white flowers. The Romans and Egyptians considered the mallow a delicacy to eat, but it was also used as a medicine to treat coughs and digestive problems. The root extract is still used to

make the Middle Eastern snack known as halva.

If you boil marsh mallow, it yields a sticky substance that you can whip into a foam. Mix that foam with honey and you can make a confectionery, which is the ancestor of our marshmallow. French cooks later refined the recipe, making it sweeter and fluffier by adding more honey and some egg white. Then they got rid of the mallow root entirely and substituted gelatin to get that firm-but-light texture.

The American food industry took an interest in the marshmallow in the 1950s and turned the snack into a product that could be made at a factory in huge amounts. Today, most marshmallows are extruded from nozzles in a long tube and then cut into pieces. The egg whites have disappeared from the factory version, but the other ingredients haven't changed too much. The spongy consistency comes from mixing sugar, water, air, and some kind of protein—usually gelatin—with a dash of vanilla and lemon for flavouring.

The second s'mores ingredient is chocolate. Cocoa beans are originally from the Amazon, but humans liked them and cultivation spread north. In Mexico, the Aztecs usually consumed chocolate as a drink. Horrified Spanish onlookers claimed the Aztecs added red herbs to their chocolate drink so it looked as if they were drinking blood.

Although the Aztecs occasionally added honey to their chocolate beverage, they usually preferred to take it unsweetened and bitter. The Spanish conquistadors didn't enjoy cocoa at first, but because the chocolate was highly valued by the Central American peoples, they threw some cocoa beans on the ship and took them back to Europe.

Europeans spent a while trying to figure out what to do with this luxury drink that nobody much liked. They tried adding honey. It helped. Then they sweetened the chocolate more, using sugar, and the drink became more like the cocoa many people drink today. That's when it took off in popularity.

But for years, *chocolate* only meant a high-end drink. It wasn't until the mid-1800s that the British company Fry's had the odd idea of turning the sweet drink into a solid bar of dark chocolate with a creamy centre. It may sound obvious today, but back then it must have seemed strange, like manufacturing a bar of solid coffee or tea.

Happily, the mixture worked. Fry's Chocolate Cream became very popular and was the first of countless chocolate and candy bars. A few years later, the Swiss added powdered milk to produce the first milk chocolate—and that will go very nicely in your s'mores.

The final s'mores ingredient is graham crackers.

The Reverend Sylvester Graham was a Presbyterian minister from Connecticut, and he would not have approved of s'mores around a campfire. He thought gluttony was almost as great a sin as alcoholism.

Even by the standards of his day, Graham was very strict, and there were many things he didn't approve of. Eating meat was one. He noted that Adam and Eve lived in the Garden of Eden eating only plants, and they lived long lives, so it was clear to him that following a similar diet would promote health, morality, and longevity.

He didn't like white bread either. Instead, he promoted his "Graham flour" in its place. It was made from coarse-ground whole wheat and could be used to make bread and, for special occasions, "honey biscuits"—the first graham crackers. He theorized that the crackers would keep young people from thinking about sex.

A cholera epidemic was raging in Europe, and Graham put the blame for that squarely on diet. He said the Europeans were drinking too much alcohol and eating too much meat and white bread. If people would only follow his sensible advice on diet and clean living, he claimed, they would be immune to cholera.

Many people thought Graham was a nut, but when cholera reached the shores of North America in the 1830s, terrified citizens flocked to his cause, spreading the popularity of his food products.

The strict diet didn't work too well for Reverend Graham. He was a sickly man for years and finally died at the age of fifty-seven. But his views on meat launched a vegetarian movement in the United States that continues to this day, while his honey crackers became very popular as a snack; for use in a pie crust, or most importantly, for creating an outer layer for our s'mores.

Today, s'mores have become a nostalgic campfire ritual, something many North Americans enjoy and some have surprisingly strong feelings about.

In 2022, *The Great British Bake Off* gave its contestants the challenge of making s'mores. The host, Paul Hollywood, sandwiched a marshmallow between chocolate and two digestive biscuits, then seared the concoction with a butane torch to avoid any mess.

The North American public, many of whom were fans of the show, were appalled. Lines had been crossed. What were these imposter s'mores? "An abomination," said some. "Criminal!" said others. And one even denounced Paul Hollywood's right to live among civilized people: "Sir, you are a monster!"

S'mores may be fireside fun, but it seems we take that fun very, very seriously.

OUT ON THE EDGE

"I got ya buddy, I got ya."
—RALPH JOYCE

Lark Harbour is a pretty place to call home—although less than a thousand people do. The Bay of Islands—where Lark Harbour can be found—is considered one of Newfoundland's best-kept secrets, and a popular network of hiking trails showcases the remote beaches, towering cliffs, and panoramic views of the Gulf of St. Lawrence.

On the morning of February 7, 2019, John Parsons had been puttering in the kitchen of his house, not too far from the beach, when he glanced through the window and noticed a seal out on the ice. He figured it would make a great picture, so he grabbed his camera, bundled up against the cold, and headed out, hoping to get a good shot from the Bottle Cove trailhead. In the parking lot, he happened to meet up with Ralph Joyce, not an unusual occurrence since Ralph walked twice a day in the area, sometimes with John and sometimes without. They decided to hike to the trailhead together. A good decision if ever there was one.

Although that morning was chilly, the week before had been mild and rainy. The two men noticed grass showing through the snow here and there as they walked to the point, which overlooks the cove from atop a rugged thirty-metre cliff. Stepping carefully, John inched out past where the grass left off, trying for a better view. He didn't notice that the ground—normally a mixture of sand, rock, and gravel—was covered by a solid sheet of ice.

"My feet came out from under me, I went on my back. And I was on my back sliding down, down [toward the edge of] the cliff," John says. "About two feet from the edge, there was a small rock sticking out. And that rock held up against my foot on the left side—my boot—and I was there on my back. And Ralph was standing there, and he said, 'My God, don't move, don't move.'"

Ralph had been a few feet behind John on the trail when John lost his footing. It was a terrifying sight, watching his friend slip towards the edge of the cliff, and for a moment Ralph feared the worst. But when he realized that John had somehow managed to stop his slide, he knew he needed to do something. And fast. He turned and headed back as quickly as he could go, shouting to John to stay calm as he went. He knew he didn't have time to go all the way to the parking lot and drive out for help, so he racked his brain for another plan.

The trail had rope along some of the walkways, so that was an option—and the best one he could come up with at first—but he knew that even getting to the rope might take too long. Desperate, Ralph stopped to catch his breath and look around for a tool he could use. There were plenty of trees nearby, but any branches on the ground were frozen into the earth. Nevertheless, it was his best hope. Ralph dug out a strong-looking stick, about four metres long, and dashed back to where John had fallen.

"I peeped down to make sure that he was still there," Ralph says. Miraculously, John was in the same spot—that small rock the only thing stopping him from plunging over the cliff and into the icy waters below.

John had never been so glad to see another person in his life. "I said, 'Ralph, my God don't let me go, don't let me go,'" he says.

"I got ya buddy, I got ya," Ralph replied as he extended the branch to his friend.

The next part was tricky. Ralph was smaller than John, and he needed leverage—which was in short supply on the icy surface. He shoved his foot against a nearby rock, braced himself, and started to pull.

"As he was pulling me up, when my foot came off the rock, that was a scary moment because there was nothing to hold me," John says. "If the tree broke or Ralph couldn't hold me or didn't have the strength I was probably gone." A few moments later, both men were back on solid ground.

After making his way home and telling his wife, Sharon, all that had happened, John went back to the trail and hung a warning sign near the cliff's edge. Later that day, when Ralph came by to check on his friend, Sharon practically lifted him through the door in a bear hug.

Sharon and John knew that Ralph deserved to be recognized for his efforts, so they didn't waste any time in filling out a nomination form for the province's bravery award. In July of 2020, in the midst of the COVID-19 pandemic that caused lockdowns and physical distancing all over the country, a small ceremony was held on the Parsonses' deck overlooking the spectacular scenery of Bottle Cove. Member of the House of Assembly Eddie Joyce (no relation to Ralph), standing in for Lieutenant-Governor Judy May Foote, presented Ralph with his award—a framed certificate and a medal featuring a stylized image of the province's trademark rugged cliffs and ocean waves.

Ralph was honoured to receive the award, but more thankful, really, for the fact he was able to help when it counted. "The main thing was I got him out of it," he says. For his part, John was thrilled when he and Sharon learned their nomination had been successful. "It's absolutely wonderful to know that his bravery on that day and his courage and his strength literally saved my life," he says. "I just don't know how to thank the man for it other than to live the best life I can and maybe help someone down the road at some point in time."

John has done his best to put the events of February 7, 2019, behind him. The outdoors is a big part of his life, and he has no intention of locking himself inside on cold or rainy days. He still hikes, although he's promised Sharon to use a tether if he's on the cliffs in inclement weather.

Ralph hasn't been so quick to get back on the trails. There are too many reminders that it could just as easily have ended badly, or that it could have been him instead of John teetering on the edge.

"I could have went on just as well as him," he says. "I didn't think about that at the time."

Although they don't meet up on the trails as often as they used to, the two are still linked. "Every time I see Ralph, there's something inside of me that says, 'This chap saved my life,'" John says. "We're connected," he adds, "and we will be connected for the rest of our lives because of what happened that day."

THE GHOST ROAD

Even in the daytime, the place has a lonely, mystic feel.

Back in the 1960s—some say earlier—a young man wanted to take his motorcycle for a night-time ride. He drove out into the country and across the marshy roads leading to Scugog Island. After cruising along the quiet rural roads for a time under the starlight, he came to a side road. It was a gravel track, long, narrow, and shrouded in black shadow, running straight south as far as he could make out. On a dark night, an unlit gravel road in the country was a dangerous place to test the limits of a motorbike, but the rider was young and foolhardy, and he wanted a challenge.

He turned onto the sideroad, feeling the motorcycle wheels crunch on the dirt. Leaning low over the handlebars, he rolled on the throttle. The engine roared, and the bike took off down the long road.

The route ahead was shrouded in total darkness, save only for the narrow beam of his headlight. The road stretched out before him, grey fading to black.

He squinted ahead as the wind blasted into his face. On either side, he caught glimpses of ditches and looming black trees, sometimes hearing a swish as a branch came close, or seeing a rabbit dart into the bush. He accelerated faster and faster, and the speedometer needle crept higher. The rider gripped the handlebars with all his strength to keep control.

And then—disaster. As he was reaching top speed, his headlight suddenly shone on something ahead. It was another road, crossing his. A split second later, the rider realized with horror that his own road ended at that same intersection.

He braked hard and tried to turn, but the velocity of his bike made the manoeuvre impossible. His motorcycle instantly went into a spin on the loose grit and flipped. The rider was thrown violently from the bike, and his head struck a large rock near the intersection. He wasn't wearing a helmet, and he was killed instantly.

His ghost still haunts the road he took that night, and his lights can still be seen travelling that highway.

This "Ghost Road" lies on Scugog Island, just a few kilometres east of Port Perry, Ontario. Today, the Ghost Road is known as the Mississaugas Trail, and it runs south to intersect Pine Point Road, where it comes to an abrupt stop—the site where it's said the deadly accident occurred. The rock is still there on the northeast corner, in front of an old wooden fence. The rock is covered with graffiti. Kids have decorated it with a pentacle.

Everyone in the area knows the story. A horse farm adjacent to the intersection gives a sly nod to the ghost story with its name—Spirit Run. Even in the daytime, the place has a lonely, mystic feel.

But those who want to encounter the ghost must wait for night. There are no streetlights here. As the sun sets, the area sinks into darkness. A nearby line of trees against the horizon looks for all the world like a long funeral procession against the fading sky. As the darkness grows, even those trees disappear into the blackness.

When the darkness is total, travel up that gravel road a way, then look back in the direction of the fatal accident. You might see a flickering red light. They say it is the red tail light of the motorcycle, hovering above the road, endlessly repeating its doomed journey.

Or you may see the white headlamp of an old motorcycle, shining in your direction, flickering over the asphalt. The light just waits, as if the dead rider is hesitant to take another ride along the road that killed him. But those who drive back to investigate will find nothing—the light simply fades away, and the intersection is empty and deserted.

The light doesn't always wait. Sometimes the experience is more frightening. The light speeds forward, coming closer and closer, tearing by the parked car of an observer. The light is white as it approaches, then changes to red as it fades into the distance. It might seem like any other vehicle, except that only the lights are seen—the motorbike and its rider are invisible. As it passes, vehicles shake. Some have reported car electronics going crazy—locks refusing to unlock, or moving on their own. Some witnesses also say the strange events were accompanied by the sound of a motorcycle far away—or long ago?

Many locals are skeptical of the story. If the crash really happened, nobody remembers it. They say the mysterious motorcycle sounds are just birds or the hoofs of horses. As for the lights, they're just ball lightning or an atmospheric disturbance—some kind of mirage probably.

About forty years ago, a group of researchers put the mirage theory to the test—one group drove to a point far south of the road, while another group, carrying walkie-talkies, waited on the Ghost Road to see what they could observe. They theorized that lights beyond the line of sight would be curved by a layer of warm air, creating the illusion of a phantom light hovering over the road. The group in the car shone their lights north. Sure enough, on the Ghost Road, the waiting observers saw a hovering light. It seemed like the big mystery was finally explained—that is, until the group with the car turned the headlights off. The observers on the Ghost Road still saw the eerie light shining in their direction, watching—and waiting.

If you visit the site, go carefully. Those dark roads may have live ghost hunters as well as dead ghosts. And if you dare to visit the rock late at night, treat it with respect, lest you anger the spirit who died there. It is said that those who sit on the boulder with an irreverent attitude may feel an angry presence behind them—and then feel themselves suddenly being shoved to the ground by a pair of invisible bony hands.

RIGHT PLACE, RIGHT TIME

"You can never underestimate the current."
—REBECKA BLACKBURN

June 20, 2018. It had been a pretty typical day for eighteen-year-old Rebecka Blackburn. A thirty-minute drive from her home in Leduc, Alberta, to the Devon Community Pool, stopping for a coffee on the way. Six hours on deck as a lifeguard, and another hour in the water teaching swimming lessons. She'd clocked out, showered off, and was thinking about what the evening might hold when she saw a message from her mom, Irene Blackburn, inviting her to join a few friends enjoying the warm evening on the shore of the North Saskatchewan River. Near Devon, the shoreline and river bottom are rocky and the currents swift, which makes the North Saskatchewan a less than ideal spot for a swim. Still, locals and visitors head for the water when the weather cooperates, eager to catch a breeze, wade in up to their knees, or on calm days, inflate a raft and float for a bit. A few minutes later, Rebecka was dressed and on her way.

Rebecka arrived at the river at about 7:15 p.m. She quickly found her mother at the water's edge—there weren't too many others at the shore that night—pulled up a lawn chair, and sat down. They'd been chatting for fifteen minutes or so when something out on the water caught Rebecka's eye.

"I looked out at the river and noticed a man quite far out splashing awkwardly," she recalls. "I brought it to my mother's attention and asked if she thought he was okay." At first, Rebecka didn't think there was anything to worry about. The man's friends were nearby, laughing and making fun of his awkward-looking swimming. It seemed like they were just fooling around. But when the current pushed him closer, Rebecka heard him yell for help. Her instincts instantly took over.

"I kicked off my flip-flops and started running into the river in his direction," she says. Her mother's friend Sommer King followed her in, along with one of the man's friends, but the strong current made them both stay where they could stand. "One of his buddies—he admitted he wasn't the greatest swimmer," Rebecka recalls. "I was like, 'You stay here, I'm going out.' I would say it was about seventy-five metres, trying to go diagonally across the river."

She swam in a head-up front crawl towards the man, keeping her eyes on him the entire time. She was just over a metre away when he stopped struggling and went under. She remembers thinking, "Oh my gosh, here we go." Once again, she didn't hesitate. Drawing on the lessons she'd learned while training to become a lifeguard three years earlier, she dove down, grabbed his body, and performed a hip carry as she turned to make her way back to shore.

Like Sommer and the man's friend, Rebecka had noticed the strong current as she swam out to where the man was flailing in the water, but it wasn't until she was pulling him to safety that she really felt the effects. "At this point, my legs were numb from exhaustion," she recalls. "The man was pushing down on me for support, and I had never felt so weak and vulnerable in the water."

She kept going, though, pushing herself forward until she was finally able to touch down. As Rebecka struggled to regain her footing on the rocky bottom, Sommer was there to assist. Together,

they brought the man to shore, where he regained his breath. The whole rescue, Rebecka figures, took ten minutes at most.

Because he was conscious and breathing, emergency responders were not called, though Rebecka suggested he seek medical attention in case of secondary drowning—a potentially fatal condition that can occur when water has been inhaled into the lungs. Later that night, one of the man's friends reached out on Facebook to say the man hadn't gone to the hospital, but he seemed to be fine. "Thanks," the message concluded, "you were a hero today."

She is without a doubt comfortable in the water—"very strong and well-trained," she acknowledges—which is why she didn't hesitate to wade into the North Saskatchewan River to rescue a drowning man. Even with her lifeguard training, though, the day's events were shocking. "I have never experienced a rescue that was as scary or intense as this one," she says, "and I'm thankful my training kicked in to autopilot. I was completely taken aback when I fatigued so quickly . . . even with the immense adrenaline that I had pumping through my body, I still have never felt so exhausted swimming in such a short period of time." It was overwhelming to feel so "attacked" by water—the element that usually brings her peace—and to wonder whether she'd be able to make it

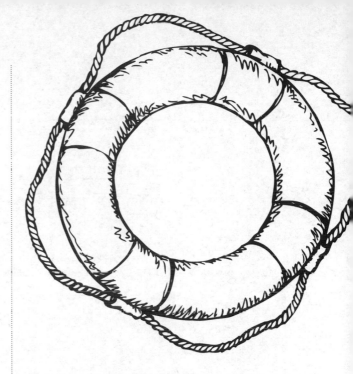

back to safety. "It just goes to show that no matter how strong of a swimmer you are, how confident you are in your swimming skills, you can never underestimate the current and the strength of it."

In the weeks and months following the rescue, Rebecka's actions were recognized with numerous awards and honours. The Red Cross Rescuer Award was, she says, "surreal," given that she'd been a member of the organization since she was fifteen years old. The Carnegie Hero Award—which Sommer King also received—was especially humbling, as it's given to only a few Canadians each year, men and women who have done extraordinary things. The Leduc Citizen of Distinction Award was special too and made her feel that the people in the city she calls home supported and were proud of her. But it was the Lifesaving Society Rescue Award that really stood out. Awarded by Lois Mitchell, the lieutenant-governor of Alberta, and presented to Rebecka in a formal ceremony alongside members of the RCMP, it helped her recognize that her calm and professional response to a dangerous situation had indeed been special.

When reflecting on that evening, she says, "I did not even think about what I was doing. I just reacted and did what needed to be done." In fact, it wasn't until she got home that night that the gravity of the situation hit her. "I was very emotional as I replayed the incident over and over again in my head and thought of all the ways it could have ended differently." Today, she thinks about it every time she crosses the High Level Bridge on her way into Edmonton and looks down on the churning waters of the North Saskatchewan River. She knows her quick thinking and strength led to a happy ending, but not a day goes by that she doesn't remember the strength of the current, the weight of the man she carried on her hip, and how weak she felt in the water. "Every time I drive across that river I am brought back to that moment of pure exhaustion and fear," she says. "It was definitely a scary situation, but I am proud of myself for not hesitating and for trusting my training to save a life."

"DID YOU HEAR THAT? I THINK IT'S
COMING FROM INSIDE THE WALL."

—Still Awake

FATHERLY FISH

Largemouth Bass

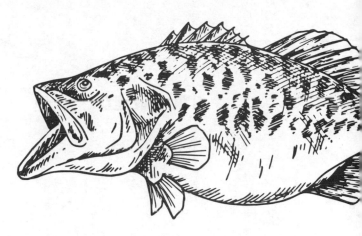

Largemouth bass are well known and prized sport fish across Canada. Native to central and eastern Canada, and particularly plentiful in the south of these regions, these fish are distinguishable from their smallmouth relations by a jaw that extends past the eye.

Adult largemouth bass have few predators; sometimes only human anglers threaten the full-grown fish. Young largemouth, on the other hand, are vulnerable to many predators, from birds like great blue herons and kingfishers to other fish like northern pike and muskellunge (muskie). To protect their eggs, male largemouth bass create nests on the lake bottom from gravel or sand and fiercely defend their territory. When a male finds a mate, the two fish swim in circles around the nest, angling their bodies so that the eggs and sperm meet on the way down. Once the nest contains thousands of fertilized eggs, the male will chase away the female and continue to guard the nest for up to ten days, until the fry hatch. The baby fish remain in schools under Dad's watchful eye for a month or so, when they are finally ready to swim out on their own.

Largemouth bass will repeat this spawning process two or three times per spring, producing tens of thousands of tiny fish. Unfortunately for the protective papas, only a fraction of a percent of these babies will grow to adulthood. But those that do can live up to twenty-five years and raise hundreds of thousands of their own little hatchlings.

WILDLIFE

STRANDED

Mallard Ducks

Mallard ducks are the most widely distributed species of dabblers in Canada, and they are most plentiful in the Prairie provinces. These ducks are unique among pond dwellers because a large portion of their diet comes from grains. When barley and wheat ripen in late summer and early fall, the mallards make flights to the fields to feed.

But mallards are one bird whose flight plans are cancelled more consistently than a low-cost airline's. Their seasonal moult takes place at a similar time as the grain harvest. Shortly after breeding season, mallard drakes (males) lose their distinctive mating plumage of shimmering green on the head and glossy blue on the wings. They shed all their flight feathers at the same time, so they are flightless until new ones appear. Females go through this same moult later, after they have finished caring for their chicks. For about a month,

mallards are grounded, living like Tom Hanks in *The Terminal*, unable to take to the skies. The ducks hide in vegetation and among reeds until they regain the ability to fly.

The feathers that appear, called eclipse plumage, are very similar in appearance for both sexes and are not much different from female breeding plumage. It is in eclipse plumage that mallards will make the winter migration to warmer climes. In spring, mallards will be the first species of duck to return to Canada, in their emerald green and sapphire blue finery once more.

TAKING A BITE OUT OF RABIES

Foxes

Foxes are undeniably adorable, from their cute little pointed faces to their bushy red tails, but like all wildlife, they have the potential to transmit disease. Foxes (Arctic and red) are one of four reservoirs of rabies in Canada. Foxes, skunks, raccoons, and bats can all carry the virus, which allows rabies to persist despite human and pet vaccination. Most mammals are susceptible to rabies, and the disease will occasionally cause outbreaks (or "spillover events") in species outside the big four. Even though rabies is rare, even among carrier species, its presence in Canada is still a public health concern because it is extremely fatal. Very close to 100 percent of people who contract rabies in North America die without vaccination.

But there is another way to prevent rabies: wildlife immunization. The province of Ontario uses an oral rabies vaccine, administered through bait traps, to control rabies strains found in foxes and raccoons. The vaccine bait they use was developed in the province and is effective at controlling the incidence of rabies outbreaks, especially when combined with targeted trap-vaccinate-release programs. Although this is cause for celebration, few other provinces have found similar success.

Bats, for whom there is no practical vaccination method, are the primary rabies reservoir in most other areas of Canada. However, only 5 percent of bats tested are positive for the virus, which indicates a much lower incidence in the larger Canadian bat population. (Only suspicious bats are submitted.)

Rabies remains a small, yet appreciable, risk of human–wildlife encounters. Be rabies aware. Never approach or handle wildlife, and be especially wary if an animal seems bold or unafraid.

LOCATION, LOCATION, LOCATION

Rabbits and Hares

In Canada we have cottontails and hares—five species of Leporidae in total. Snowshoe hares, Arctic hares, and jackrabbits make up Canada's hares, who have longer legs and bigger ears than their fellow buns. But the most "punny" distinction between the two types is that rabbits are born naked, while hares are born with *hair* (well okay, fur). You can also tell the difference between a rabbit and a hare by where it lives. Rabbits burrow, while hares nest above ground.

And location doesn't just distinguish hares from rabbits: it should also distinguish Canada's two types of cottontails from one another. Eastern cottontails and mountain cottontails each live in their eponymous regions of Canada . . . for the most part. Eastern cottontails are common in Ontario, Quebec, and Manitoba. Mountain cottontails are found in British Columbia, Alberta, and Saskatchewan. And never the twain shall meet, right?

Wrong. Eastern cottontails were introduced to mainland British Columbia in the 1920s and Vancouver Island in 1964, and they have bred like, well, you know.

The eastern cottontails' diet of young vegetation is harmful to delicate habitats, especially those found on Vancouver Island. They are considered an invasive species, proving once again that location is key in everything from cottage choice to bunny lovability.

MORE THAN
MEETS THE EYE

Squirrels

Every cottage has a squirrel. Some people give them cute nicknames and happily watch their treetop antics. Others fight with their squirrels over birdfeeders and destruction of property. But few cottage owners realize just how many doppelgangers pose as "their" squirrels. Maybe you can distinguish two or three individuals by size or markings, but did you know that up to twenty-five squirrels might live in the square kilometre near you? If there are mature trees and human residences, squirrels have more abundant food and fewer encounters with predators, so their population can soar.

Cottagers are sometimes baffled when they try to remove problem animals. "Identical" squirrels keep appearing after trapping and relocation efforts, even prompting some owners to mark caught squirrels to distinguish them from new vandals. Others, with a more lethal approach to squirrel control, are agape as trap after trap is set and sprung, with seemingly no end in sight. Squirrels can have two litters of up to seven babies each year, so it's no wonder there's an army of them in the trees.

Some adjustments that can help keep the peace include using plastic pipes on buildings and metal collars on trees and poles to discourage climbing, metal storage bins for pet food or birdseed, and squirrel-repelling scents near gardens or in attics (like hot pepper, vinegar, or mothballs). Prevention through squirrel-proofing strategies like these is probably best because, at the end of the day, there will always be more squirrels.

BUILDING
A DEATH STAR

Beavers

How do beavers construct their lodges? Maybe they follow similar blueprints to the Empire's planet-sized Death Star in *Star Wars*. Beavers build their lodges in the middle of a pond or other body of water, often one they created or enlarged themselves by damming a creek or stream. The lodge is in water deep enough to resist freezing to the bottom, so the beavers can swim in and out to get food from their various caches all winter long.

The ice above and the frozen dome of woven branches and packed mud make the lodge almost impenetrable to attack. However, like the infamous exhaust port on the Death Star, beaver lodges have one point of above-water vulnerability: an air vent. If you watch a beaver lodge on a cold, clear winter day, you may even see cloudy puffs of condensation emerging from the conical top of the lodge, as the beaver family within breathes.

Few of the beaver's predators are small enough to take advantage of this weakness, and ever fewer are willing to face the wrath within—adult beavers can be 1.3 metres long and weigh more than thirty kilograms, with wickedly long, curving teeth sharp enough to fell trees. There have been instances of beavers attacking dogs at off-leash parks, so coyotes are understandably wary, preferring to surprise a lone beaver while it is out foraging. In fact, the only animals who regularly threaten the young beavers and kits inside the lodge are otters, who can enter from the water while the frightening adults are away.

RETURN OF THE JEDI

For over two centuries, European colonizers waged a one-sided war on beavers. They were systematically hunted and trapped for their pelts, valuable for making fashionable hats, until there were no beavers to be found. In the winter of 1928–1929, a trading post near Waskaganish, Quebec, was able to produce only four beaver pelts, despite trapping efforts that covered 25,000 square kilometres. By the 1930s, zoologists were grieving the inevitable extinction of the beaver. Somewhat prematurely, as it turns out.

Today, beavers have rebounded to a population estimated at twenty million, returning to Canadian waterways through successful conservation and reintroduction programs. The return of the beavers restores wetlands and revitalizes ecosystems.

And we need beavers to thrive because their activities raise the water table, protect against drought, and conserve the movement of fresh water through the North American watersheds.

But human–beaver tensions still simmer beneath the surface. When beavers steal fence posts, cut Internet lines, or flood towns, it seems like guerilla warfare: rebel beavers versus the human Empire. In truth, people are just living on land that was long ago engineered by beavers, but our own engineering has failed to take them into account. Moving forward, the challenge is to keep nature and ecosystems at the forefront of our designs for cities and society: to create a built environment that functions in concert with the natural world, rather than seeking to dominate it.

CITY SLICKERS

Coyotes

Most animal populations suffer from urbanization and development, but some adaptable species flourish when humans change the landscape. Although both wolves and coyotes were persecuted and killed relentlessly throughout the European colonization of Canada, only wolves have lost ground: coyotes have expanded their range and grown downright metropolitan.

Because coyotes are smaller than wolves, they can thrive on the rodents and small mammals that cities have in abundance and easily find dens that are warmer and more secure than those readily available in rural areas. Coyotes are also extremely flexible in their diet and social behaviours, eating anything from grasshoppers and fruit to refuse and carrion, and living in groups or solo depending on resource availability. In fact, coyotes are quickly becoming a vital part of stable urban ecosystems, and they rarely pose a threat when people practise good wildlife coexistence strategies.

If coyotes live near your cottage, consult your municipal or provincial parks website to familiarize yourself with local regulations and recommendations, but general guidelines include removing or securing potential food sources, closing up access to potential den sites (like under stairs, decks, or sheds), keeping pets properly supervised or leashed, and lightly hazing any coyotes that seem too comfortable near your property (by shouting, popping an umbrella, throwing things, etc.). Never feed coyotes. Wild animals are safest when they are kept wild, even when found in the heart of a city.

PRICKLY FOREST RANGERS

Porcupines

With 30,000 sharp spikes armouring its body, the porcupine is an easily recognizable feature of Canadian wildlife. And while you probably know that reports of porcupines shooting their quills are false—the quills are simply loosely attached to their skin and can be easily dislodged when the porcupine swings its tail at a threat—you might not realize these large rodents are experts in sustainable forest management.

Although they were once thought to be destructive to forests because their habit of munching on new growth and young saplings kills some trees, when the porcupine population is in proper balance, their grazing actually supports forest health. They eat "weed" trees that would choke out other species and thin out saplings like a proficient gardener thins out their carrot crop. They also enjoy eating parasitic mistletoe off of trees—but maybe hold off on giving them a yuletide thank-you kiss, or you might end up with a porcupine quill lip piercing!

Better to leave the quill decorations for the beautiful traditional garments, textiles, and quill boxes created by Indigenous Peoples across Canada. According to the Whetung Ojibwa Centre, the quills they use are often collected from roadkill.

Porcupines are particularly susceptible to traffic accidents because they have poor eyesight and move slowly. Drive carefully to avoid porcupine collisions, especially after dark when the animals are most active.

YOUR LOONY
LOONIE

Loons

Common loons have far from common features. For one, they have solid bones. Most flighted birds have hollow bones, but solid bones allow loons to dive deep under the water to catch fish, snails, and other aquatic treats. Loons also have red eyes. This feature is caused by a pigment in the loons' retina that enhances its underwater vision, like a light filter. And loons' webbed feet are placed further back on their bodies than many other water birds, which gives them more power when they are diving and swimming underwater.

All these adaptations add up to a bird that is most comfortable when in the water—indeed, loons rarely leave the water except to nest or fly. When taking to the air, loons require a longer runway than similarly sized birds, and they are downright awkward when walking on land. This makes loons uniquely vulnerable when they are nesting, so they always choose waterfront property. Prime locations include partially sunken logs, small islands, floating mats of vegetation, and muskrat lodges.

Loons are a federally protected species, and their nests are of particular concern in conservation efforts. Nests can be easily swamped by boat wakes, and shoreline development constricts available nesting sites for the already selective birds. Floating artificial nesting platforms, constructed from PVC piping, waterproof floating foam, and sod and plant matter, have proven successful in lakes where loons had previously failed to hatch and fledge.

If you are concerned about the loons in the waterways near your cottage, you can join the citizen scientists with the Canadian Lakes Loon Survey to monitor the health of the loon population near you.

THE LOON'S TUNE

Common loons are known for their beautiful, haunting calls. In fact, loons have four distinct calls, which they use in different combinations to communicate with their families and other loons. The first is the *tremolo*, a wavering sound that is given when the loon is alarmed or wants to announce its presence. The *yodel*, an expression of aggression, is the male's territorial claim. The *wail* is the haunting call that reminds us of summertime in cottage country. It's frequently used during social interactions and to determine location. And finally, there's the *hoot*, a call of curiosity or happiness, used mainly by family members to stay in touch with each other.

 WILDLIFE

FROM TRASH PANDA TO WASH-BEAR: WHO IS THAT MASKED BANDIT?

Raccoons

Raccoons are easily recognizable thieves with their black masks and black-banded tails. Since they are agile, nimble, and omnivorous, they thrive easily in the wild and near human habitation. The only requirements for raccoon residence appear to be food, water, and small enclosed spaces to den in, so they are found across southern Canada. Newfoundland and Labrador is a notable exception: raccoons are not native to the island, but conservation officers trap one or two freight-container stowaways per year.

Elsewhere, frequent human–raccoon interactions have led to numerous aliases and appellations for the nocturnal mammals. The common English name *raccoon* is probably derived from the Algonquin word *aroughcoune*, which roughly translates to "one who scrubs with its hands." This washing behaviour of raccoons has led to names internationally too. *Waschbär* in German, *orsetto lavatore* in Italian, and *araiguma* in Japanese all translate to "wash-bear." In a slight variation, modern French speakers in Canada and abroad call the animals *raton laveur*, or "washing rat." But early Canadian French more accurately captured the nature of the urban raccoon with its term *chat sauvage*, or "wild cat." Although baby raccoons may enjoy people, adult animals are typically standoffish and aggressive. The Internet has also taken a crack at naming the adaptable little menace, who is equally at home in a tree stump and a garbage can—hence the nickname "trash panda."

SMELLY KITTENS

Skunks

Did you know that baby skunks, or "kits," can make their signature scent at birth? It takes a few months before juveniles can spray with accuracy, but even the babies can give off a whiff of malodour. The scent is produced by glands at the base of the tail and can take weeks to wear off.

Effective remedies for skunk spray range from a mixture of vinegar and laundry detergent to a concoction of hydrogen peroxide, baking soda, and dish soap. The effectiveness of bathing in tomato juice to remove the stink, however, is just an urban legend. It only overwhelms your nose so that all you can smell is tomato juice. The skunky smell will remain once the tomato juice is long gone.

If a skunk burrows near your cottage, you might smell it long before you ever glimpse the black-and-white striped or spotted animal itself; skunks are nocturnal. Popular places for a den include under porches, decks, stairs, and sheds. You might find skunk tracks, like tiny bear prints with five clearly defined toes, in freshly dug earth. You will rarely see skunk tracks in snow because skunks are inactive for weeks at a time in winter.

If you need to remove a skunk, they can be easily live-trapped, as their smelly defence lends itself to a nonchalant attitude. (Skunks have few predators outside of owls, who have a poor sense of smell.) Once you catch a skunk, be sure to cover the trap with an old blanket and move it slowly and quietly, to avoid setting off a stink bomb. Skunks need to be relocated at least four kilometres to prevent their return.

CANADIAN COBRA CHICKENS

Canada Geese

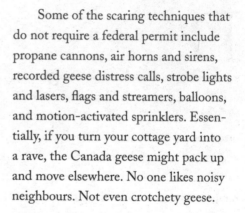

Many of us have a love–hate relationship with Canada geese. We know they are one of the most recognizable symbols of Canada, at home and abroad. They are also vicious miscreants. From the kilogram per day of poop that each goose lets loose, to the trademark hiss that earned them their Internet moniker of "cobra chickens," our geese can be a real pain. And during nesting season, their aggressive tendencies can disrupt people's daily routines, keeping people from reaching their mailboxes, sitting on their favourite park benches, or enjoying a walk outside.

Some consider the annoyance an honour, as these waterfowl were on the verge of disappearing entirely at the turn of the twentieth century. Others find that tangling with the weight class of "beat extinction" is a little too much, preferring to keep nests and geese off their properties.

Some of the scaring techniques that do not require a federal permit include propane cannons, air horns and sirens, recorded geese distress calls, strobe lights and lasers, flags and streamers, balloons, and motion-activated sprinklers. Essentially, if you turn your cottage yard into a rave, the Canada geese might pack up and move elsewhere. No one likes noisy neighbours. Not even crotchety geese.

BEE THE CHANGE YOU WANT TO SEE

Bees

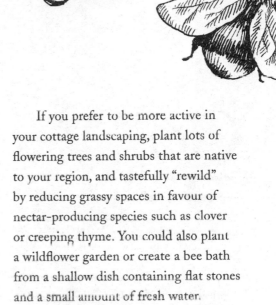

You may have already heard that the bees need our help. But did you know that domesticated honeybees, though famous, are not actually native to Canada? These sweetener producers were brought over from Europe in the 1600s, and their care and management are best left to apiarists, as honeybees cannot survive in the wild here.

The more than eight hundred species of bees who do live in the Canadian wilderness are in more danger. Wild bees suffer when their habitats are lost or damaged, but your cottage can become a haven. One of the easiest ways to protect native bee habitats is to be lazy. Mow the lawn less frequently. Let fallen logs lie for a couple of seasons. Don't spray pesticide or herbicide. Don't clear dead plant debris before winter. Simple acts of sloth like these provide homes for wild bees and protect them from harmful chemicals.

If you prefer to be more active in your cottage landscaping, plant lots of flowering trees and shrubs that are native to your region, and tastefully "rewild" by reducing grassy spaces in favour of nectar-producing species such as clover or creeping thyme. You could also plant a wildflower garden or create a bee bath from a shallow dish containing flat stones and a small amount of fresh water.

Another popular option is to create a bee "hotel" from rolled cardboard or holes drilled into blocks of wood. Use these with caution and plenty of research. Although bee hotels can be helpful when carefully constructed, fungus, mould, and predatory wasps may make them unsafe for wild bees if they are not well maintained.

WILDLIFE

ANTLER ANTICS

Elk, Deer, or Moose?

Common animal names can be confusing, especially when people from diverse languages and cultures get together. Different cultural and language traditions each have their own names for the animals in their region, and sometimes these names overlap and intersect in puzzling ways. One of these "Who's on first?" quandaries occurs in naming members of the Cervidae (deer) family. Here in Canada, we call the largest member of the deer family *moose*, but in England a similar mooselike species is called *elk*. In Canadian English, elk are smaller than moose but larger than what we call *deer*, generally white-tailed or mule deer.

So if you are speaking to someone most familiar with British English, they might be wondering why you are calling the largest deer a moose and not an elk, while you are perplexed about where the elk is while you are looking at a moose.

And which ones are the deer, dear? They're all types of deer! On balance, it might be safest to do what the scientists do to avoid confusion: use the Shawnee name *wapiti*, meaning "white rump," to describe that majestic medium-sized deer we Canadians know as *elk*.

STILL CONFUSED? HERE'S A DEER DEETS SHEET

Deer (in Canada, usually white-tailed or mule deer)

All animals in the deer family have four legs, hooves, and a coat that is some shade of brown, and the males have antlers for at least part of the year. White-tailed and mule deer are relatively small; although white-tailed bucks can weigh up to 200 kilograms in their northern ranges, mule bucks rarely weigh over 95 kilograms. White-tailed deer are easily identified by the white fur on the underside of their tails, which they raise when alarmed. You'll see the white tails bouncing and bobbing away from you into the trees. Mule deer's most distinctive feature is their extra-large ears, which tend to resemble the ears of a mule, earning them their moniker.

Wapiti (in Canada, commonly known as elk)

Wapiti are larger than either mule or white-tailed deer, weighing up to 350 kilograms as a matter of course, with exceptionally large bucks weighing in excess of 500 kilograms during breeding season. From a distance, their rumps look white, which earned them their Shawnee name, but on closer inspection the colour is closer to ivory, with an orange tinge to it.

Moose (in Canada a moose is a moose, but not across the pond!)

Moose are the largest animals by far, with bull moose weighing 600 kilograms, and a Yukon subspecies weighing up to 800 kilograms. Moose look awkward; they have long, slender legs topped with a barrel-like body and chest. Appearances are deceiving, though: moose move gracefully through even the deepest snow and step easily over most fences. If you can't identify a moose by size alone, the males' antlers have flat, palmlike surfaces that the points extend from (unlike deer and wapiti antlers, which tend to be slim and pointy throughout), and most moose have a bell, or strip of fur-covered skin, hanging down from their throats.

WILDLIFE

SANTA'S NOT-SO-LITTLE HELPERS

Caribou

Did you know that caribou are reindeer? Or maybe reindeer are caribou. Either way, reindeer and caribou are the same species of deer: *Rangifer tarandus*. Although there are many subspecies with distinctive characteristics, in Canada we call all the wild animals (and the ones that appear on our quarters) *caribou*, which likely comes from the Mi'kmaw word *xalibu*, and the domesticated ones *reindeer*.

So are there any reindeer herds in Canada? You bet! Aside from the reindeer owned by the big man in red himself (who couldn't be reached for comment), the most famous Canadian reindeer herd can be found near Inuvik in the Northwest Territories. This herd was brought to Canada from Russia in the 1930s in a five-year globe-trotting pilgrimage, facilitated by Sami herders and Alaska natives. Introduction of these reindeer was necessary after the local caribou popula-

tion died out because of human (European colonizer) impact. The reindeer travelled by steamship, railcar, and hoof to reach their current home in the Mackenzie Delta. In 2021, an Inuvialuit organization took over management of the herd, whose animals are key to strengthening food security and food sovereignty in the region. The herd ranges in size from 2,200 to 2,800 reindeer, a mix of males, females, and calves.

A full-grown male can reach 250 kilograms, but you may not be able to tell smaller males and females apart for much of the year: both grow antlers. Cows keep their antlers all winter long, but bulls shed their antlers long before Christmas. So Santa's 120-kilogram sleigh pullers are all female!

CARIBOU IN CRISIS

The Indigenous Peoples of Canada have lived with caribou herds since time immemorial, hunting, and sometimes moving, in rhythm with the herds' migrations and seasons, nurturing a spiritual connection with and deep reverence for these animals. Such balance and respect allowed hundreds of thousands of caribou to thrive on the land, and other plants and animals flourished as a result: wildlife ecologists consider caribou an "umbrella" species, which means their heath and continued presence protect the ecological space for thousands of other vital plants and animals, from lichen and insects to wolves and trees.

Today, caribou numbers have decreased by up to 90 percent for many herds, and some have disappeared entirely. This causes a butterfly effect that ripples outwards through interconnected plants and animals, causing irrevocable damage.

Despite monumental efforts by Indigenous Peoples and other conservationists, caribou populations continue to decline.

It's not enough to merely cull wolves or maintain the current protected lands. Threats to caribou come from many different quarters, from clear cutting and oil and gas production to climate change and habitat loss, and revitalization must come through a fundamental shift in how we Canadians steward the environment as a whole. If we want to have caribou anywhere besides on the change in our pockets, it's long past time to practise the respect and listening that was present on the land thousands of years ago.

BATS NEED SUMMER COTTAGES TOO

Bats

The nineteen species of bats that spend time in Canada are notoriously inept at placing online bookings, but many of them need a cottage rental over the summer months. This is because Canadian bats tend to spend their winters in more southerly climes or underground, where the temperatures remain above freezing. In these overwintering sites, bats mate and hibernate, but it's not until temperatures climb that they seek places to give birth and nurse their babies. These summer vacation rentals are generally found under the bark of trees or inside gaps and hollows in the trunks.

But when trees are cleared to make space for people cottages, or diseases like white-nose syndrome affect the bat population, the bats need new, safe places to spend their summer days. Enter bat boxes. These human-made bat cottages give tired bats a place to roost after a night of eating thousands of bugs (including *mosquitoes*).

If you are eager to "eat into" your local mosquito population, why not try hosting your own bat B&B? Information on how to build and mount a bat box can be found on the Bat Conservation International's website or on the Ontario Parks blog. Once your bat hotel is up and running, consider joining in bat box research and monitoring through your local bat conservation group or a nation-wide project like WCS Canada's BatBox Project. Information from your bat box can be helpful for conservation efforts and public recommendations for bat box design in Canada.

"OH, GO JUMP IN THE LAKE!"
—Vexed on Vacation

Campfire Stories

KEEPING THE WOLF FROM THE DOOR

*"I felt like I had kind of punched someone
that was way out of my weight class."*
—Russell Fee

If you're looking for a scenic spot to pitch a tent and spend a few days, you can't go wrong with Alberta's Banff National Park. Nestled amid the awe-inspiring Rocky Mountains, the UNESCO World Heritage Site is a nature lover's dream. There are turquoise glacier-fed lakes to paddle and endless trails to explore. Whatever the season, visitors from all over the world flock there, with an average of four million guests each year.

Matthew and Elisa Rispoli and their two boys travelled to the park in the summer of 2019. On August 9, the family from New Jersey had spent the day swimming, skipping rocks, and enjoying the beauty all around them. That night, they returned to their tent in the Rampart Creek Campground, worn out. By midnight, they were fast asleep.

One tent site over, Calgarian Russell Fee and his wife were also tucked in for the evening. The campground was quiet. And then the screaming started.

At first, fuzzy with sleep, Russ figured a child had gone missing. But something about the desperation in the voices, the calls for help, told him otherwise. "The screams were so intense that I knew it was obviously a terrible situation," he says. "Panic immediately sets in."

Russ unzipped the flap of his tent and fumbled with his shoes as his wife handed him a lantern. Moments later, he was dashing in the direction of the screams. As he neared the campsite, a strange and horrific scene came into view: the tent was a shredded mess, and sticking out of it was the hind end of a wolf—larger than any dog Russ could ever recall seeing. The animal had something clamped in its jaws that it was attempting to drag. "Just like he's pulling on a toy," Russ recalls. He quickly realized that that "toy" was the arm of the man in the tent.

Russ didn't even break stride. "I had a good run going at the time . . . and it was just so quick and the screams were so

CAMPFIRE STORIES

intense . . . so I just kind of kept running at it and I just kicked it sort of in the back hip area."

More startled than hurt, the wolf let go of the man's arm and backed out of the tent. But it didn't run away. As it stared at him, Russ wondered, for the first time, if he was in over his head. "I felt like I had kind of punched someone that was way out of my weight class," he says. Before he had time to think, Matt—scratched, bitten, and bleeding—charged out of the tent after the animal. "He was pretty amped up, too, so we both just started screaming at it."

When the wolf attacked, Matt had thrown himself between the animal and his family. Elisa Rispoli had lain down on top of the kids to protect them, as Matt did his best to fight off the wolf. As it tried to drag Matt away, Elisa had grabbed hold of her husband's legs. "We were screaming for help as he was fighting it and trying to save us, for what felt like an eternity (but I think was anywhere from 1–3 minutes)," she later wrote in a Facebook post. "[It was] like something out of a horror movie." Russ's arrival—and his swift kick to the wolf's back end—created the distraction the family needed.

As Matt and Russ threw rocks at the wolf to try to scare it off, Elisa and the boys made a frantic dash for the safety of the Fees' minivan.

"It didn't even really seem terribly aggressive, which is a weird thing to say," Russ Fee says. "I did make contact with a couple of rocks, and it didn't even seem to care. It was just doing the perimeter of the site, back and forth, staring at us."

Eventually, the wolf backed off enough for Matt and Russ to join the others in the van. The Fees drove the traumatized family to a nearby hospital for medical attention. The rest of the night, Elisa wrote, was a "blur of EMTs, good Samaritans, waiting for treatment, no phone service, and crying." Matt needed rabies shots but was otherwise okay. If not for their "guardian angel," she added, "it could have been so so much worse."

Wolf attacks on humans are extremely rare. In fact, the Rispolis' experience was the first incident of its kind in a Canadian national park (there have been attacks reported in provincial parks, but only twice). In the aftermath of the attack, Parks Canada evacuated the campsite until they were able to track down and euthanize the wolf. It was, park officials reported, in extremely poor health, which was likely a factor in the strange behaviour it exhibited. There was nothing found at the campsite that would have attracted or provoked the animal.

Whatever led the wolf to behave in such an uncharacteristically aggressive way, there's no question that Russ's arrival on the scene prevented tragedy. The Rispoli family certainly knows it, and on July 1, 2020, Governor General Julie Payette announced that Russ would be awarded the Medal of Bravery for his actions. Since ceremonies were not being held during the COVID-19 outbreak, Payette used her Facebook page to introduce some of that year's award recipients. On August 13, it was Russ's turn. Under a summary of his actions on that terrifying night was a quote from Russ himself: "My advice would be to prepare for all of life's challenges, both the expected and the unforeseen. Rarely do you get a say in how they'll arrive, but we all must handle them eventually."

The Rispolis understand this better than most. Russ is prone to downplaying his actions that night, telling those who ask that "it's never felt right to call it brave because I didn't know what I was getting into." He was, he says, "just going to help some people and didn't realize the severity of the situation."

But Elisa isn't willing to brush off the part Russ played in protecting her family. "We are forever grateful to Russ who came to our aid and likely saved Matt's life," she wrote. The family also isn't willing to let the attack colour their feelings about Banff and the wonderful adventure they'd been having before things took such a terrifying turn. In an Instagram post a few days after the encounter with the wolf, they wrote: "The Lakes in Alberta and BC are amazing, the mountains are dynamic, the wildlife is (well you know). Even though half of our trip has been focused on getting our lives back together I still find it stunning up here . . . I'm sure I'll be back someday but maybe in a camper van instead."

LIKE A DOG WITH A DRONE

This was the worst time to be distracted
by bright lights and a yappy dog.

Canada's gun laws are much stricter than those in the United States. It's particularly difficult for Canadians to get hold of the kinds of small, easily concealed handguns favoured by criminals. That means there's money to be made smuggling pistols from America to Canada. But if you get caught at the border, you're in trouble.

Gunrunners have tried many approaches. They have hidden guns inside the gas tanks of cars, and they have attached them secretly to the vehicles of unsuspecting tourists. (The smugglers track down the cars later and remove the illegal packages.)

But, in a modern twist, a group of smugglers in Michigan hit on what they figured was the perfect approach: they would use drones. A big drone could just about carry fifteen pounds, which translates to ten or eleven average-sized pistols. The state of Michigan is separated from neighbouring Ontario only by a river in many places. It's a good place to sneak something across.

On April 29, 2022, around 4 a.m., the American gunrunners went to a point on the US side of the St. Clair River and attached a bag holding eleven guns to a $7,000 drone. The drone had been modified for covert use: its lights had been disabled so it couldn't be easily spotted.

The drone's operator, "Tom," was at the controls on the Canadian side. As far as we can tell, he'd driven his pickup truck to the planned landing spot, about twenty-five kilometres east of the Detroit suburbs.

Once the drone was loaded with weapons by his colleagues on the American side of the St. Clair River, his partners signalled him, and he launched the vehicle.

The trip over the river was fairly short—less than a kilometre. With the weight of the guns, the battery life of the drone was being pushed to the limit, but Tom had accounted for that. It was all going perfectly.

The area had many trees, but Tom had chosen an open area for the landing spot—the backyard of a house situated beside the river in the little town of Port Lambton, about forty kilometres downriver from Sarnia.

Tom congratulated himself on the flying. Weather conditions were good—not too much wind. Now, as he carried out the most difficult part of the operation, landing the drone, he needed all his attention. Not that there would be many interruptions. That's why he'd chosen four in the morning for the transfer—he wasn't likely to be interrupted by anyone.

But he was wrong about that.

According to the *Globe and Mail*, the occupant of the house near the landing spot was woken by his little Yorkshire terrier, who felt a pressing need to "go outside." The bleary-eyed owner dragged himself out of bed and opened the door for the dog.

But as the homeowner looked down towards the river, he noticed movement in his yard. This was weird. Someone was out there, trying to stay hidden. He shone a flashlight towards the figure and called out. The little dog bounded out to investigate.

Tom was trying to get the landing right, and this was the worst time to be distracted by bright lights and a yappy dog. It threw Tom off his game. The drone, instead of landing, swerved to one side and found a nearby tree. And it got stuck there.

Tom panicked. He didn't want to risk a ten-year sentence for gun trafficking. He ran for his truck and sped away, leaving behind his $7,000 drone, which was carrying a bag of guns he could have sold for $22,000 to criminal buyers in Toronto. The drone and its cargo were picked up soon after by the Ontario Provincial Police.

Police are still working on technology to protect against smuggling by drone. In this case, though, a low-tech approach worked just fine. The criminals were unable to do their business—because the dog wanted to do his.

MOSQUITOES

If a mosquito lands on a person and narrowly escapes being swatted,
it will remember the smell of that person and avoid them in future.

Who doesn't hate mosquitoes? Even many people who say they "wouldn't kill a fly," who carefully transport spiders and centipedes out of the house, will swat a mosquito without mercy. When your enemy is trying to eat you, the gloves come off. But we're up against a cunning foe.

Only female mosquitoes bite humans. They need nutrients from the blood of animals, and they can't produce eggs without them. But the rest of the time, the female mosquito has a decidedly sweet tooth, dining on nectar from plants. The male mosquito eats nothing but this nectar.

Male mosquitoes may not suck our blood, but that doesn't mean they're not interested in you and me. If you find a mosquito hovering around you but never landing, it could well be a male. A 2021 study showed that male mosquitoes are attracted to humans almost as much as the females are. It seems to be all about

finding a mate. The females will be drawn to people, and if the males fly around us, they have a better chance of connecting with a well-nourished girlfriend.

Mosquitoes are very stealthy and can use various techniques to sneak up on you without being caught. And they are alert to threats. By day, they depend on their excellent vision: they can see in all directions, and if they spot an approaching hand, they take evasive action with a power dive. At night, some species use a different approach. They fly in an unpredictable way, which makes them extremely hard to hit.

The small size of the mosquito is another factor that makes it a difficult insect to kill. If you bring a hand down towards a resting insect, the approaching wall of air may knock the lightweight mosquito sideways before it gets crushed. If you're stalking a mosquito that's resting on a flat surface, try to hit it with the palm of your hand rather than the edge—that's where the approaching air current is most stable and least likely to blow the insect to freedom. Better yet, use a swatter with a meshlike surface. A flying mosquito can sometimes be killed by clapping two hands together so the mosquito is caught between the palms.

We've all cursed mosquitoes that get away, but insect experts say even a near miss can be useful. Amazingly, mosquitoes quickly learn to avoid danger. If a mosquito lands on a person and narrowly escapes being swatted, it will remember the smell of that person and avoid them in future.

These pests are good at hiding and will often land in shadows and under ledges. Placing a flashlight flat against a wall and shining it sideways can extend the mosquito's shadow and make its location more obvious.

One of the distinctive things about mosquitoes is the way they lift their long hind legs after they land. It is thought they are using their legs like antennae, sensing movements in the air that might flag danger, while their heads are buried in your skin.

You might find you've been bitten without being aware of it. That's because a mosquito can make not only a soft landing but also a discreet getaway. Most insects launch themselves into flight by pushing off with their legs, jumping into the air, and then flapping their wings. If the mosquito did that after feeding, their host might notice the movement and swat it. So, instead, the mosquito keeps the touch of its legs very delicate and uses only rapid wingbeats to rise into the air.

There are a few things you can do to avoid being bitten. One is to stay clear of other people—the less carbon dioxide is in the air, the less attractive the area is to mosquitoes. The cloud of carbon dioxide from a group of people is very attractive.

If you're indoors, turning on a fan can mix up the carbon dioxide and create chaotic air currents, making it much harder for a mosquito to find you and land.

It's well known that mosquitoes are attracted to dark shades, so wearing white should reduce your chances of mosquito bites nearly as much as it increases your chances of a mustard stain. But it's not a black and white issue—a recent study suggested that, after getting a whiff of carbon dioxide, mosquitoes also home in on some colours more than others. They are particularly attracted to red, orange, black, and cyan but uninterested in green, purple, blue, and white. Unfortunately for us, the reddish colour of human skin—regardless of pigment—is one of the mosquito's favourite hues.

Some studies suggest that drinking alcohol makes you more attractive to mosquitoes. Or do you just *feel* more attractive?

If you eat plenty of foods from the onion and garlic family, that may keep the

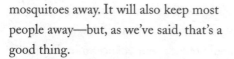

mosquitoes away. It will also keep most people away—but, as we've said, that's a good thing.

Plenty of creatures eat mosquitoes, especially swallows and purple martins. There are even some insects that prey on mosquitoes. Dragonflies and damselflies have fantastic eyesight and can catch mosquitoes on the wing. And they are even better mosquito exterminators when they are young. The wingless larvae of both insects live in fresh water and are ferocious predators of mosquito larvae.

You may have seen a crane fly performing a messy flight around a window, looking like it doesn't know what to do with its long, trailing legs. Crane flies look a little like giant mosquitoes, but they are not closely related and are harmless to humans. Some people call crane flies "mosquito hawks" or "skeeter eaters" and

believe they eat mosquitoes, but it's not so—they are harmless to mosquitoes too.

It would be great to have a reliable way to stop mosquitoes from biting us. Technology may have a solution. A company called Bzigo is developing a mosquito tracking system. When its camera detects a mosquito, the device shines a laser in the mosquito's direction. Unfortunately, the laser doesn't shoot the mosquito from the air, but it does highlight the location of the mosquito so a human can kill it.

The company says that future versions of the device may both detect and kill the mosquito. Once that arrives, you can sit in your cottage without worrying about protecting yourself from mosquito bites—although you may need to protect yourself from potshots by the household laser.

THE GHOST OF THE FAIRY LAKES

The landscape might have natural beauty,
but it was no place for a farmer.

There are several Fairy Lakes in Canada, and at least two of them are said to be haunted.

One is situated in Gatineau Park in Quebec, just northwest of Ottawa. Lac des Fées is the site of an Algonquin legend. The story goes that, centuries ago, before the arrival of Europeans, a beautiful Algonquin woman was admired by two warriors. The men were strong and charming, and she was attracted to them both, favouring first one, then the other, but unable to make a final choice between them.

One day, the community was alerted to the approach of some rivals. The warriors gathered and prepared to fight. Even now, she could not choose between them. She watched with dread as both her lovers left for the battle. What if one of them died? But perhaps this situation could resolve her indecision. If one warrior died in battle, she would marry the other.

The fighting went on all day, and by the end of it, the enemy had been driven off, but a thousand warriors lay dead. The woman went looking to see which of her two lovers had survived. Neither one had. She was so overwhelmed with grief that she threw herself into the lake and drowned.

According to the legend, her spirit still haunts the lake, as a figure in white. It's said that the spirits of the two warriors also haunt the place, but although the woman's spirit can see the warriors, they cannot see her. They hunt back and forth around the lake, searching for their lost love, while she watches from the water, forever unable to reach them or help them.

* * *

Another Fairy Lake is situated in Ontario, near Huntsville. This lake is also haunted by a ghostly figure. It is sometimes seen wandering the area. And there are sounds too—a distant wailing, a cry of unimaginable sorrow. The story behind the haunting is more recent than that of the Fairy Lake in Quebec but no less sad.

In the 1800s, the British Empire wanted Canada to be settled. The land, much of it occupied by Indigenous Peoples, was carved up and assigned to settlers. These new immigrants were expected to remove any trees and begin farming—if they failed, they would lose their land. Officials drew boundaries on a map, often without knowing much about the nature of the land they were giving away.

Settlers who were given land in some parts of the country could do very well. The Niagara Peninsula was well suited to growing fruit. The southwest of the province, down towards Windsor, was warmer in climate and particularly good for growing corn.

But other areas were not so friendly to farmers. One of the reasons Ontario's "cottage country" retained its natural feel was that farming there was so difficult. Glaciers had scraped their way across the land as they had retreated, leaving a trail of lakes and rocks. Nature had not had much time to build up a thick layer of soil, and what was there was poor. The landscape might have natural beauty, but it was no place for a farmer.

One couple were given land east of what is now Huntsville. They did what they were instructed to do—cleared the trees off their plot, built a log house, and started to farm. They started with high hopes and worked hard, but the land did not cooperate. Crops didn't want to grow there.

The wife had a child, a girl, but gradually became worn down by the hard work. She became sick and died.

Father and daughter both grieved at their loss. Perhaps the farmer should have given up then and found a different place to farm, or returned to his homeland, but he couldn't do it. When the grieving was done, he worked harder than ever, and his young daughter followed his example. She wanted to please her father and did her best to carry on the work her mother had performed. The farmer admired his daughter's spirit and determination.

Indigenous Peoples still lived in the area. They watched the farmer's efforts with incomprehension. Why was he trying to grow food here? they asked him. This was no land for crops—it could provide other bounty. There was good fishing, good hunting, and good trapping.

They were right. The farmer worked hard, scratching at the thin soil, trying to get something to grow, but if anything grew at all, it was small and stunted or quickly died. He didn't grow enough to sell—or enough to feed his family.

But he didn't starve. As the Indigenous community had said, both hunting and fishing were good there, and even though the farmer was not skilled in these areas, he could find enough to feed himself and his child through the summer and fall. He even killed a bear, eating its meat and using the pelt for a carpet.

But as fall moved into winter, their supplies ran low. Both father and daughter were getting thin. Each day, the farmer went out with his gun, but the weather was bad, and it seemed as if all the animals were hiding. He spotted a deer and took a shot but missed, and the animal bounded away. On another occasion, he pulled the trigger but the snow-soaked gunpowder was too wet to fire. Time and again, he returned home empty-handed.

Finally, the day came when their food had run out entirely. Again, the farmer left his daughter in the cabin and went out to hunt, but now he was both desperate and determined. He told the girl, "This is the last day you will go hungry."

He wandered through the forest and criss-crossed the lake as the snow whipped around him. Again, he found nothing, but he refused to give up, so he stayed out longer. He remained out all day.

At home, his daughter was weak with hunger. She stared outside, wondering what had happened to her father. Had he fallen? Did he need help? Would he ever return?

He was still out there, trudging through snow, still trying to feed them both. The sun was setting in the west when he suddenly saw what he was looking for. An animal was moving across the frozen lake. The farmer crouched down behind a tree and kept still. He had only one shot, and it could be the difference between life and death for himself and his daughter. He took careful aim and pulled the trigger. His flintlock fired. The bullet hit its mark. The animal fell dead.

He whooped with relief and delight. He stumbled forward across the lake to retrieve the carcass, to bring home the meat that would save their lives. But as he drew closer, he saw with horror that the dead body before him was not that of some wild animal. It was his own daughter. She had gone out to look for her father, wrapped in the bearskin rug.

And since that day, it's said that, if you travel to Fairy Lake in winter, you may see a figure, like a small animal, moving across the lake, and hear the distant cries—a girl eternally looking for her father in the snow, and a father eternally grieving the loss of his child.

BEAR-KNUCKLE FIGHTING

Ruff did what any Canadian homeowner would do—put up his dukes and sparred with the huge animal.

A 2021 YouGov survey asked Americans which animals they thought they could defeat in unarmed hand-to-hand combat. Nearly 40 percent didn't fancy their chances against a goose, and close to a third thought they might be defeated by a house cat or a rat.

But at the other end of the confidence spectrum, 6 percent of women and 7 percent of men were confident they could use nothing but determination and a sweet pair of fists to defeat a grizzly bear.

Could they be right? In a word, no. Experts say an unarmed human is probably not going to defeat any kind of bear, never mind a 300-kilogram grizzly, but they might just put up enough of a fight to make the bear back down. Some Canadians have found that out.

A Muskoka homeowner named Norman Ruff noticed that some of his garbage cans and bird feeders had been knocked over. It was clear that bears

had been busy around the house, but he never saw a live animal. That changed in July 2019, when in the early hours of the morning, the eighty-year-old man heard a commotion coming from his kitchen. He went down to investigate and discovered a male black bear that had pushed its way into the kitchen and was now unable to get out of the house.

The bear gave a colossal roar and reared up onto its hind legs, its head reaching nearly to the ceiling. Ruff did what any Canadian homeowner would do—put up his dukes and sparred with the huge animal. He said he got several good punches to the bear's nose—"the only place I could reach."

The fight continued for twenty minutes. In that time, while his wife called 911, Ruff managed to get the front door open and was trying to steer the bear towards it.

The bear was able to get some swipes in and gave Ruff's hand a bite. Finally, it

seemed to have had enough of the fight and left through the open door.

Ruff was taken to hospital and had surgery to reconstruct his thumb. The hospital staff were amazed to hear the cause of the injury was a bare-handed bear fight. The senior later received an award for bravery from the OPP.

✻ ✻ ✻

In June 2016, Rick Nelson, a sixty-one-year-old resident of Sudbury, had an outdoor encounter with a bear. He was out walking his dog when he came across a bear cub. He wasn't alarmed, but the baby bear was—it gave a distress call, and moments later the bear's mother had charged onto the scene and reared up in front of Nelson, swinging its great paws.

Nelson was experienced as a boxer and used all his skill to avoid the blows. He noticed that the bear fought like a right-handed human—a swing with the left, then a much bigger swing with the right. Nelson picked his moment and landed an uppercut on the bear's snout.

The bear backed down and left with its cub. Nelson breathed a sigh of relief that the bear had walked away from the fight, leaving him with just scratches across his chest and face. In his words, he "really lucked out."

✻ ✻ ✻

Many bear victims are taken by surprise, but some people go looking for trouble. In 2015, two experienced nature photographers were taking photos of a grizzly in Banff National Park when a red pickup truck arrived on the scene. Two men got out of the truck. Both seemed like they'd been drinking. One man, Devin Mitsuing, was a professional chuckwagon driver from Saskatchewan. Now he appeared to have his heart set on a fight.

He threw rocks at the bear, seemingly trying to taunt it, then pulled off his shirt and took a boxing stance. Now it was bear versus bare-chested.

Mitsuing yelled and taunted the bear for some minutes, then ran at it. Fortunately for him, the grizzly decided not to bother fighting this oddly aggressive man and instead trotted off into the woods.

The photographers reported the incident to the RCMP, who arrested Mitsuing. He was later convicted of disturbing wildlife in a national park and fined $4,000.

* * *

A man in North Vancouver found a novel method to stop a bear attack.

Chris Springstead was outdoors sipping a mug of coffee when he saw a black bear digging into a neighbour's garbage. Just as he saw the bear, the bear saw him.

It put its head down and walked purposefully towards him.

Springstead knew it would be unwise to run, so he raised his arms and tried to look big.

The bear was not impressed and charged at Springstead, rearing up in front of him. At that point, the man smashed the porcelain coffee mug down on the bear's head. He smashed it down a second time for good measure. This time, the mug shattered.

The mug shot did the trick. The bear ran off into the bushes, awed by Springstead's fighting skills. That, or it didn't like his coffee.

HUNTING THE HUNTER

*He was certainly aware that he'd done some cross-border shooting
when he crossed the border himself and posed for photos.*

"Marcus" was a hunter from Fairbanks, Alaska. In August 2017, he was hunting near the Canadian border when he spotted a Dall sheep, a wild animal that likes to live in mountainous areas. The sheep is mostly white, with large, curling horns. The animal was a very desirable target for a hunter, and Marcus was licensed to shoot one in Alaska.

Yukon News reported that there was one small problem: the sheep wasn't in Alaska. It was across the border, on the Yukon side, in Canada.

Marcus took aim and killed the sheep.

A wide band of cut trees marks the boundary between the two countries, but Marcus later claimed he hadn't realized the sheep was more than a hundred metres away, on the other side of the border, when he shot it.

Whether that claim is true or not, he was certainly aware that he'd done some cross-border shooting when he crossed the border himself and posed for photos with the dead sheep. He used the usual hunter trick of holding the head close to the camera, so the dimensions of his victim were exaggerated and it looked as though he'd brought down a beast the size of a moose.

He then dragged the sheep back to the American side, butchered it, and took the parts he wanted back home. He checked in with US authorities, telling them that the sheep had been killed in Alaska, although he knew full well it was shot in Canada.

Marcus posted his pictures on a Facebook sheep-hunting group (there's a group for everything, isn't there?) and bragged about shooting a "Yukon zebra"—referring to the dark markings on his sheep. The Dall sheep with these markings is sometimes called a Fannin sheep.

It seemed like he'd avoided being caught for cross-border poaching, but the act caught up with him the following year, when an anonymous tipster sent copies of Marcus's photos to Canadian officials, suggesting that this American hunter had been killing Canadian animals.

The officials who monitor illegal hunting go to considerable lengths to investigate these reports, and they were soon on the case. They took a helicopter to the area where Marcus had killed the sheep and explored it, trying to find an exact match for the landscape in his photo. This was no small task. The photo showed only nondescript rocky hills and a few tiny trees. But at last, they found the precise spot and took a photo to match the one taken by Marcus. They marked an arrangement of ten small features—little trees, small ridges on rocks. Individually, none of the features would have clinched the case, but when they were viewed together, the new photograph showed conclusively that Marcus's earlier photo had been taken in Canada. It was an impressive sleuthing job.

Marcus was charged with unlawful hunting and unlawful export. The crimes could carry heavy fines, from $5,000 up to $300,000.

In his favour, when Marcus was confronted with the charges, he cooperated and pleaded guilty. He also handed back his trophy, the mounted head and shoulders of the dead sheep. In court, he asked for the minimum fine: $5,000.

The prosecutor agreed he'd been cooperative, but wanted to deter other trigger-happy hunters. He asked for a $12,500 fine and a five-year hunting ban.

The judge compromised—Marcus wasn't a wealthy man, so she gave the hunter a five-year ban and an $8,500 fine. Of that money, $7,500 went to the Yukon's program for tipsters.

The remaining $1,000 went to the one person who profited from Marcus's crime: the person who turned him in.

THE GHOST CANOE

She was shocked when the boat simply vanished.

Tom Thomson is one of the best-known Canadian artists. He painted pictures of Ontario's wilderness that perfectly capture the feeling of the area—the vast skies, the lakes, the pine trees permanently bent by the wind into eerie shapes. His evocative work and style inspired the Group of Seven.

Thomson didn't begin painting seriously until his mid-thirties. He took a train trip from Toronto to a little place called Canoe Lake in Algonquin Park. One glance at his new surroundings and it was love at first sight for Thomson. He camped there and fished. He took his canoe out onto the water. But perhaps most important, he started painting the landscape. His work was astonishing and inspired. Art experts liked what they saw, and Thomson quickly went from an unknown artist to a rising star. He seemed to have a mystical connection with the wilderness.

Every year, he returned to Algonquin Park. When Thomson wasn't painting or sketching the Algonquin Park landscape, he was enjoying the experience of life among the trees and lakes. He got a guide's licence so he could show other visitors and tourists around the land he loved.

He was becoming more productive than he had ever been, and he was getting wider recognition. But it was all about to come to a tragic end.

In the summer of 1917, Thomson took his canoe out for a trip on Canoe Lake, the first place he'd come to when he arrived there, and still one of his favourite locales. He didn't return. Later that afternoon, someone spotted his overturned canoe. There was no sign of Tom.

His body was not discovered for more than a week. The official pronouncement was an accidental drowning, but some people had doubts. Rumours swirled about people who might have wanted Thomson dead—an angry creditor, an aggrieved lady friend, a jealous husband.

Fishing line was wrapped around his ankles. There were signs of injuries to his head. Some said there was a bullet hole. Others noted the haste of Thomson's burial. Later, his body was exhumed and reburied in a family plot, but there was speculation it was not the same body, and that something about the death had been hushed up. Had he been murdered out there on the lake?

Rumours of a supernatural kind also emerged. Those who looked at Thomson's art had always felt Thomson had a spiritual connection with the lakes and forests, but soon after his death, they started finding a spiritual connection of a different kind. One woman was heading for shore in her canoe when she spotted another canoe coming out to meet her. The occupant looked like Thomson, wearing the same kind of yellow shirt as he had died in, and he paddled in the same style too. She called out to him. She was shocked when the boat simply vanished.

Other witnesses reported seeing similar sights, usually in the morning when the mist still covered the lakes. The phantom often appeared as a lonely figure in a yellow shirt, paddling a grey canoe that was there one moment and gone the next. But some encounters were more ominous.

Jimmy Stringer was a longtime resident of the Canoe Lake area. He was interviewed by a journalist for *Macleans*

magazine in 1973. Jimmy was seventy-three by then, but as a young man, he remembered meeting Tom Thomson, and he remembered seeing the artist around the area—noting not just his face but also the way he moved, his distinctive way of paddling.

Stringer grieved as much as anyone when the artist died. But his dealings with Thomson were not over.

Some years after Thomson's death, Jimmy Stringer was accompanying a group of Americans who had come to Canada for a two-week canoe trip. Others in the group had gone on ahead, and Stringer was in the canoe with one of the tourists. Suddenly, the American became alarmed—he started screaming and looked terrified. Jimmy asked what was wrong. The American said, "Didn't you see him?"

The American described how a figure had been talking to him, saying his brother had drowned at a mill. Jimmy Stringer had seen and heard nothing. He asked what the person looked like. The American described the figure. "He was tall, long black hair, wearing a yellow shirt . . ." A chill ran down Stringer's spine—it sounded like Tom Thomson. They continued down the river and came to the mill. The other members of the party were there, desperately diving into the water. There had been a terrible accident, they said. The American's brother had drowned.

Jimmy Stringer claimed he'd also seen the ghost himself. It happened early one morning. Stringer was out on the water—the lake was densely shrouded in mist. Suddenly he saw a grey-green canoe pull up close beside him. Stringer turned and saw a man grinning at him. He recognized the face immediately—it was Tom Thomson. As Stringer stared back in astonishment, the figure and the canoe simply faded away.

What did it mean? Jimmy Stringer didn't know. He wondered whether the ghost wanted help or needed him to get to the bottom of a mystery. Stringer had heard stories about the mysteries surrounding Thomson's death from the folks who had known Thomson well, and he knew a few things that hadn't made it into the records. He made plans to investigate them.

In the spring of 1973, Jimmy Stringer took his own canoe out onto Canoe Lake. He didn't come back. His friends found his tobacco pouch floating on the water. Alarmed, they searched the area. They found nothing—like Thomson, more than fifty years earlier, Jimmy Stringer had gone missing on that lake.

At last, Jimmy's body appeared, floating on the surface. Officials could only guess at what had happened. It seemed there had been some kind of canoe accident. Another "accidental drowning" on Canoe Lake. Was the ghost an omen of Jimmy Stringer's impending fate? Was this why the phantom had appeared to him?

Stories still circulate about a canoeist travelling those misty waters. If you happen to be in those parts and spot such a figure in the distance, see if he's wearing a yellow shirt. But if he's coming in your direction, turn another way. It may be better to avoid a close encounter.

LOST FOOTPRINTS

It looked like a trail.
You could follow one man the whole way.

In 1908, a team was working under Lake Ontario, building a waterworks tunnel below the bed of the lake between downtown Toronto and the Toronto Islands. There they made an incredible discovery—a procession of human footprints clearly marked in the blue clay.

Experts were called in to take a look at the find. It seemed the tracks had been left by a group of people wearing moccasins. They were travelling north. There were many prints, so it was either a large group or a well-used trail.

And the age? According to the experts, because of the depth the prints were found at and the type of clay, they must have been made around 11,000 years ago.

One astonished city inspector described the scene to reporters. He said, "It looked like a trail. You could follow one man the whole way. Some footprints were on top of the others, partly obliterating them. There were footprints of all sizes,

and a single print of a child's foot, three and a half inches."

Tiny details were perfectly preserved. You could see how the clay had squeezed around a walker's heels. The inspector said he had tried to lift a piece of the clay to keep it, but the material was so delicate it just crumbled in his hand.

The footprints revealed part of an incredible human migration. Ontario was buried under more than a kilometre of ice until 12,000 years ago, but as conditions warmed and the ice retreated, animals moved north into the new land that was exposed, and human hunters followed them. The travellers who made those footprints must have been some of the earliest inhabitants of what is now Canada. The landscape has changed greatly since then—in those days, it was kilometres from the lake, and the clay was in the middle of subarctic tundra. The moccasined walkers must have come up from what is now the United States, probably following the large animals they hunted—caribou, bison, mammoths, and mastodons. The remains of mammoths have been found at other locations around Toronto.

Finding the footprints was an incredible fluke. The prints may have been the earliest evidence of human life in eastern Canada. A newspaper article declared it one of the most important finds ever made on the American continent.

Unfortunately, in 1908, officials ranked construction ahead of archaeology. It didn't matter how fascinating these footprints were, they had a waterworks tunnel to build. So, after the experts had taken their photos and made their sketches of the footprints, the workers returned to their task and poured concrete over everything.

"HOME IS WHERE YOU HOLIDAY POUR."
—Thirsty and Thriving

Happy Hour

HAPPY HOUR

GATHERING FAMILY AND FRIENDS AT THE COTTAGE ALWAYS FEELS LIKE A BIT OF A CELEBRATION—WHETHER IT'S THE MAY LONG WEEKEND, CANADA DAY, A FRIDAY AFTER THE END OF A BUSY WEEK, OR JUST A BEAUTIFUL SUMMER EVENING.

Having fun drinks to serve and share adds to the sense of occasion, so why not try something new or mix up a batch of a cocktail that feels fancier than your favourite beer or wine? Casually pouring mojitos for a room full of people is a sure way to impress. (Plus, mojitos are delicious.)

These recipes are all guidelines and can be tweaked according to taste. So, for example, if you really like mint or you don't have a particular orange liqueur on hand, feel free to add more or substitute something similar. Also, make the most of local produce—whether it's home grown or from a nearby farmers' market or U-pick farm, you can't beat the flavour of fresh ingredients.

HOT TIPS FOR BATCH DRINKS

BATCH DRINKS ARE GREAT WHEN YOU'RE SERVING A GROUP, AND THEY'RE SUPER FAST TO PUT TOGETHER. THE RECIPES PROVIDED IN THIS SECTION ARE ALL PRETTY FLEXIBLE: ADD MORE OR LESS MINT, STRAIN OR DON'T—IT'S UP TO YOU. HERE ARE SOME TIPS TO MAKE LIFE A LITTLE EASIER WHEN MIXING BATCH DRINKS.

- WHEN INCLUDING A CARBONATED INGREDIENT IN A BATCH DRINK (E.G., SPRITE AND 7-UP WORK WELL IN A MOJITO; SEE PAGE 139), COMBINE EVERYTHING ELSE FIRST, AND THEN ADD THE CARBONATED ITEM ONLY WHEN YOU POUR A SERVING. THAT WAY, YOU WON'T LOSE THE FIZZ.

- SIMPLE SYRUP IS GREAT TO HAVE ON HAND IN YOUR BAR BECAUSE IT MIXES EASILY INTO DRINKS AND MEANS EVERYONE CAN HAVE THEIR DRINK AS SWEET AS THEY LIKE IT. YOU CAN ALWAYS ADD SWEETNESS TO A DRINK, BUT YOU CAN'T TAKE IT OUT. IT'S ALSO SUPER EASY TO MAKE AND THE RECIPE CAN BE SCALED UP OR DOWN AS NEEDED—SIMPLY DISSOLVE 1 PART SUGAR IN 1 PART WATER. IN A HEATPROOF JAR OR CONTAINER, COMBINE 1 CUP OF GRANULATED SUGAR AND 1 CUP OF BOILING WATER. STIR UNTIL THE SUGAR COMPLETELY DISSOLVES. THAT'S IT. LET THE SYRUP COOL BEFORE ADDING IT TO DRINKS. YOU CAN STORE SIMPLE SYRUP IN THE FRIDGE FOR SEVERAL DAYS.

- ALWAYS SERVE THESE DRINKS WITH ICE, BUT DON'T PUT ICE IN THE BATCH ITSELF—IT'LL WATER THE DRINKS DOWN.

MOJITO BATCH RECIPE

Mojitos are a classic and refreshing cocktail with rum, mint, and lime as the key ingredients. They look snazzy because of the fresh mint, and the flavours go perfectly with a hot day. Despite the elevated look, this is an easy drink to make, and one that lends itself well to batch mixing.

MAKES 1 BIG PITCHER

1 X 26-OZ (750 ML) BOTTLE
 OF WHITE RUM
1 BIG HANDFUL OF FRESH MINT LEAVES
JUICE OF 2 LIMES
1 TO 2 TBSP (15 TO 30 ML) GRANULATED
 SUGAR
70 OZ (2 L) SODA WATER, SPRITE, OR 7-UP

1. Place the fresh mint leaves in a bowl or a large glass jar. Add sugar, to taste, and the lime juice. Using either a muddler or the end of a wooden spoon, gently mash the mint into the juice until the mint leaves are pretty thoroughly squished and the sugar has totally dissolved into the lime juice.

2. Pour the mint mixture into a container big enough to hold the entire bottle of rum (a large jar or a juice pitcher works great). Add all of the rum, and stir well. Set aside for a few minutes.

3. To serve, add 1 to 2 oz (30 to 60 mL) of the rum mixture to a glass and top with soda water. Serve with a straw. Garnish with a sprig of fresh mint.

TIPS

- To sweeten, stir in more sugar or substitute Sprite or 7-Up for the soda water.
- Add as much lime juice as you like.
- If you prefer, you can use a cocktail strainer or small fine-mesh sieve to strain the mojito mixture as you pour to keep the mint pieces out of your glass.
- This mix will keep in the fridge for a couple of days (if it lasts that long).

HAPPY HOUR

SANGRIA BATCH RECIPE

Sangria is a great choice for when you have a bottle of wine sitting around that isn't your favourite or you want to use up something cheap and cheerful. Even a partial bottle that has to be finished will work—there's no need to use the good stuff! Don't forget to pack a ladle along with your pitcher in case anyone wants chunks of fruit in their glass of sangria.

MAKES 1 BIG PITCHER

1 TO 2 CUPS (250 TO 500 ML) SLICED FRESH FRUIT (YOUR CHOICE; SEE TIP)

1 X 26-OZ (750 ML) BOTTLE OF WINE (YOUR CHOICE; SEE TIP)

2 TO 3 OZ (60 TO 90 ML) ORANGE LIQUEUR (E.G., TRIPLE SEC OR COINTREAU)

3 TO 5 OZ (60 TO 150 ML) RUM (WHITE OR GOLDEN IS BEST) OR BRANDY

1 TO 2 CUPS (250 TO 500 ML) FRUIT JUICE (YOUR CHOICE; SEE TIP)

SIMPLE SYRUP (SEE PAGE 138)

SODA WATER (OPTIONAL)

1. Place fruit in a large pitcher. Add the wine, orange liqueur, and rum (start with the lesser quantity of the rum and liqueur—you can always add more later).

2. Add the juice and simple syrup. Taste and amend with additional liqueur and liquor, juice, or simple syrup, as desired.

3. Serve over ice. To make it fizzy, top with soda water.

TIPS

- When choosing fruit, try to select a variety. Berries, sliced citrus fruit, chunked stone fruit—anything goes. (That said, you may want to skip bananas.)
- If you want it to look pretty, cutting your citrus into wheels will add a nice touch.
- Try to consider which fruit or juice flavours will taste the best with the wine you're using: A white wine may be better suited to peaches, lemons, and kiwis. A red works best with oranges, strawberries, and blueberries. (But don't let anybody tell you what to do!)
- If you prefer your drinks less sweet, start with a drier wine, since the fruit and juice will make it sweeter.

MARGARITA

When making a margarita, the ratio of ingredients used can vary depending on your preferences, but a good start is a 2:1.5:1.5 ratio of tequila, lime, and orange liqueur. It's easy to taste and adjust from there. Please note that this is a strong cocktail with not much mix involved. It's also delicious and easy to drink quickly, especially on a hot day. Serve and consume responsibly.

MAKES 1 DRINK. TO MAKE A BATCH, MULTIPLY BY NUMBER OF SERVINGS DESIRED.

2 OZ (60 ML) TEQUILA

1.5 OZ (45 ML) ORANGE LIQUEUR (E.G., TRIPLE SEC OR COINTREAU)

1.5 OZ (45 ML) FRESH LIME JUICE

SIMPLE SYRUP, TO TASTE (SEE PAGE 138)

1. Combine the tequila, liqueur, and lime juice in a container big enough to hold them (a large jar or juice pitcher works great). You can either serve a margarita over ice (skip Step 2 if so) or shake it with ice in a cocktail shaker.

2. If using a shaker, fill the shaker two thirds full of ice. Pour the margarita mix over top, leaving at least 1 inch (2.5 cm) of headspace space below the rim. Cover with the lid and shake, shake, shake! The outside of the shaker will get frosty. As you continue to shake, little ice pieces will break off, creating a slushy effect.

3. To serve, pour the mixed drink into a glass (over ice, if not shaken), using a cocktail strainer or fine-mesh sieve to strain it, if desired.

TIPS

- Change the ratio to taste: Having tequila as the highest percentage makes it boozier. Having lime as the highest boosts the tartness and citrus flavour. Having the orange liqueur as the highest will make it much sweeter.

- For a fancier presentation, serve your margaritas in salt-rimmed glasses: Sprinkle a couple tablespoons of kosher salt on a small plate (if you have rock salt, even better). Run a lime wedge around the rim of your empty glass, wetting the edge completely. Turn the glass over and rest it in the salt on the plate. Move it around a bit to coat the rim. Carefully pour your margarita into the glass (over ice if you didn't use a cocktail shaker).

LONG ISLAND ICED TEA

Despite the name, Long Island iced tea has no tea in it—it was named for the colour. This potent drink can be made in many ways, but this is one way: 2 parts tequila, 1 part rum, 1 part vodka, 1 part gin, and 1 part orange liqueur. If you're not keen on tequila, try equal parts of all the alcohols. Remember not to add your cola to the batch—add it to each drink to keep the fizz. Serve over lots of ice and consume responsibly.

MAKES 1 DRINK. TO MAKE A BATCH, MULTIPLY QUANTITIES BY NUMBER OF SERVINGS DESIRED.

1 OZ (30 ML) TEQUILA

0.5 OZ (15 ML) RUM

0.5 OZ (15 ML) VODKA

0.5 OZ (15 ML) GIN

0.5 OZ (15 ML) ORANGE LIQUEUR
   (E.G., TRIPLE SEC OR COINTREAU)

1 OZ (30 ML) COLA

FRESH LEMON JUICE (LIME JUICE ALSO
   WORKS)

SIMPLE SYRUP (SEE PAGE 138)

1. Combine the tequila, rum, vodka, gin, and liqueur in a container big enough to hold them (a large jar or juice pitcher works great).

2. To serve, pour the mixed drink into a glass with ice. Top with cola and lemon or lime juice, to taste. Stir in simple syrup, to taste, if desired.

RHUBARB SPRITZER

Rhubarb is a sign of spring. Celebrate the opening of the cottage with a refreshing rhubarb cocktail.

SERVES 8

4 CUPS (1 L) CHOPPED RHUBARB (3 TO 4 STALKS), CHOPPED INTO ½-INCH (1.5 CM) CHUNKS

1 TBSP (15 ML) WATER

2 TBSP (30 ML) GRANULATED SUGAR

1 X 750 ML BOTTLE OF PROSECCO, CHILLED

1. Place the chopped rhubarb in a food processor fitted with the metal blade. Add the water and sugar. Process the mixture until smooth.

2. Using a fine-mesh sieve and the back of a wooden spoon, press the rhubarb mixture through a sieve into a juice pitcher or large jar. Discard the pulp. (You should end up with about 1 cup/250 mL of juice.) Cover and chill for at least 1 hour.

3. To serve, divide the rhubarb mixture between 8 glasses (about 2 tbsp/30 mL of rhubarb syrup per serving). Top with chilled prosecco just before serving.

MAKE-YOUR-OWN RADLERS AND SHANDIES

BEER-BASED COCKTAILS SUCH AS RADLERS AND SHANDIES HAVE BECOME INCREASINGLY POPULAR. THE ONLY DIFFERENCE BETWEEN A RADLER AND A SHANDY IS THAT A SHANDY IS MADE WITH LEMONADE RATHER THAN JUICE. STORE-BOUGHT VERSIONS CAN BE PRICEY OR TOO SWEET, OR YOU SIMPLY MAY NOT HAVE ONE IN THE FRIDGE WHEN YOU WANT IT. MAKING THESE REFRESHING BEER COCKTAILS YOURSELF MEANS YOU CAN CONTROL THE FLAVOUR AND EVEN THE ALCOHOL CONTENT. IT'S AS EASY AS POURING HALF A BEER INTO A GLASS WITH ICE AND TOPPING IT OFF WITH EITHER JUICE OR LEMONADE. THAT SAID, SOME FLAVOURS WORK BETTER TOGETHER THAN OTHERS. A CITRUSY, HOPPY IPA MAKES AN EXCELLENT RADLER WHEN PAIRED WITH A TART GRAPEFRUIT JUICE. YOU CAN ALSO PLAY WITH THE BEER-TO-JUICE RATIO IF YOU PREFER MOSTLY BEER WITH JUST A LITTLE JUICE, OR MORE OF AN EVEN MIX.

BEER PAIRINGS

LIGHT LAGERS: CURRIES, BURGERS, SALADS
WHEAT BEERS: SPICY FOOD, FRUITY DESSERTS
INDIA PALE ALES: STEAK, BARBECUE, MEXICAN FOOD
AMBER ALES: PIZZA, FRIED FOODS
DARK LAGERS: PIZZA, BURGERS, STEWS
BROWN ALES: SAUSAGE, FISH, SUSHI

TROPICAL BEER COCKTAIL

A fun way to dress up a glass of beer is by turning it into a tasty cocktail.
Here's a good one to try.

SERVES 1

1 COLD BOTTLE (12 OZ/341 ML) OF LIGHT
   LAGER (E.G., CORONA, SOL, MODELO)
1 OZ (30 ML) TEQUILA
ORANGE JUICE
GRENADINE
LIME WEDGES

VARIATIONS

You can substitute pineapple or peach
juice for the orange juice, and rum or
vodka for the tequila.

1. Drink a bottle of beer down to the top
of the label or pour beer into a larger glass.

2. Add tequila, and then top up with
orange juice to partway up the neck of the
bottle or to the desired level in your glass.
Add a splash of grenadine (a little goes a
long way), and then squeeze in the juice
from a lime wedge.

3. To mix, plug the top of the bottle with
your thumb and turn the bottle upside
down once. (Don't shake it—beer is carbonated and will explode.) If your thumb
doesn't cover the bottle opening, you can
also use the flat of your palm—just make
sure it totally covers the opening so nothing leaks out. If you've made it in a glass,
gently stir. Serve.

THE BLOODY CAESAR

*The Bloody Caesar, a.k.a. "Caesar," is Canada's national cocktail. It was created
in a hotel bar in Calgary in 1969. And though there are many variations on the recipe,
the building blocks are vodka, hot sauce, Worcestershire sauce, fresh lime juice, seasonings for the rim
of the glass, and, of course, tomato-clam juice (e.g., Clamato). Feel free to get creative and add your
own special twist and garnishes. This recipe is an adaptation of the classic Caesar created
in Calgary. For a non-alcoholic version, simply omit the vodka.*

SERVES 1

½ TSP (2.5 ML) CELERY SALT

½ TSP (2.5 ML) GARLIC SALT

½ TSP (2.5 ML) STEAK SEASONING

¼ OZ (5 ML) FRESH LEMON OR LIME JUICE
(FROM ½ A LEMON OR LIME), PLUS MORE
FOR COATING THE RIM OF THE GLASS

4 OZ (120 ML) TOMATO-CLAM JUICE

1½ OZ (45 ML) VODKA

2 DASHES OF WORCESTERSHIRE SAUCE

2 DASHES OF HOT SAUCE (OR HORSERAD-
ISH, TO TASTE)

SEA SALT AND FRESHLY GROUND BLACK
PEPPER

A CELERY STICK OR PICKLED VEGETABLE (BE
CREATIVE: ANYTHING FROM A DILL PICKLE
SPEAR TO A COCKTAIL PICK SPEARED
WITH A PICKLED ONION AND CARROT
WORKS GREAT)

1. Make the rimmer: in a small bowl or plate, combine the celery salt, garlic salt, and steak seasoning.

2. Frost the rim of a highball glass by wetting the rim with lime juice and then dipping it in the prepared rimmer mixture. Add a few cubes of ice to the glass.

3. Carefully pour the tomato-clam juice, vodka, Worcestershire, and hot sauce into the glass. Season with salt and pepper, to taste. Using a mixing spoon, stir well, being careful not to disrupt the rimmer. Garnish the glass as desired, and serve.

CLASSIC CANADIAN COCKTAILS

CAESARS AREN'T THE ONLY CLASSIC CANADIAN
COCKTAIL. TRY ONE OF THESE DRINKS FOR A
REFRESHING CHANGE:

- CARIBOU (BRANDY, PORT WINE, VODKA, AND DRY SHERRY)
- B-52 (A LAYERED SHOT MADE UP OF A COFFEE LIQUEUR, IRISH CREAM, AND GRAND MARNIER)
- SLOCUM MAPLE SMASH (VODKA, MAPLE SYRUP, LEMON JUICE, AND SOMETIMES A LITTLE SODA WATER)
- RAYMOND MASSEY (RYE, GINGER SYRUP, AND CHAMPAGNE)
- ANGRY CANADIAN (THE CLASSIC OLD FASHIONED WITH MAPLE SYRUP SUBSTITUTED FOR THE SUGAR)

TO FIND RECIPES FOR THESE CLASSICS, ALONG WITH ENDLESS
CREATIVE VARIATIONS, TRY A QUICK WEB SEARCH FOR THE
NAMES AND INGREDIENTS LISTED ABOVE.

MIXING MOCKTAILS

*If you're looking to make non-alcoholic cocktails
or mixed drinks, it's helpful to keep fruit juice and sodas on hand.*

FRUIT JUICE OR FRUITY SODA

SODA WATER

FRESH LIME OR OTHER CITRUS FRUIT
   (LEMON, ORANGE, GRAPEFRUIT)

GARNISHES (LIME WHEELS, MINT SPRIGS)

1. For a simple mocktail, mix fresh lime (or any other citrus) juice with your fruit juice—you can shake this mixture over ice if your fruit drink is not carbonated—and top with soda water. The type and strength of juice or fruity soda you have on hand will determine how much soda water (if any) you want to use.

2. Serve over ice, in a nice glass, and with a garnish. A lime wheel or a sprig of mint will go a long way to making your mocktail feel like an elevated drink.

TIP

To make something feel like a cocktail, you want to have some complexity of flavour. You also may want to add a flavored sugar or salt rim or serve it in a cocktail glass.

VARIATION

If you enjoy non-alcoholic spirits that mimic the taste of regular spirits (e.g., Seedlip), those are great options, too. Of course, de-alcoholized and no-alcohol wines and beers on the market have been getting better, so try some of those if that's the experience you're after.

RHUBARB LEMONADE

Served over ice, this tart pale pink lemonade is a refreshing way to welcome spring.
It can also be used as concentrate and mixed with water or soda water.

SERVES 8 (OR MORE IF YOU ADD A MIX)

6½ CUPS (1.6 L) WATER

¾ TO 1 CUP (185 ML TO 250 ML)
  GRANULATED SUGAR

4½ CUPS (1.125 L) COARSELY CHOPPED
  FRESH RHUBARB

JUICE OF 1 LEMON

1. In a saucepan, bring the water and sugar to a boil. Stir in the rhubarb and bring the mixture back to a boil. Reduce the heat to low and simmer for 5 minutes.

2. Using a fine-mesh sieve placed over a bowl, strain the rhubarb mixture—without pressing, to keep the syrup from getting cloudy—for 10 minutes.

3. Transfer the syrup to a pitcher or large jar (discard the pulp). Stir in the lemon juice.

4. Cover and refrigerate for at least 4 hours.

STRAWBERRY LEMONADE COOLER

This is a simple, pared-down version of a classic mocktail, not to mention a great way to use up really ripe strawberries! Customarily, the strawberries would be puréed in a blender, but in a basic cottage kitchen, mashing them with a fork will suffice and make cleanup super quick. The quantities below are for one serving—if serving more, just double or quadruple the recipe, as needed.

SERVES 1

6 RIPE STRAWBERRIES, HULLED AND
    ROUGHLY CHOPPED
½ CUP (125 ML) LEMONADE
½ CUP (125 ML) SODA WATER
ICE CUBES AND FRESH MINT LEAVES,
    TO SERVE

1. Using a fork or wooden spoon, mash the strawberries in a tall glass.

2. Pour in the lemonade and soda water, and stir well. Add some ice and sprigs of mint, and enjoy.

VARIATIONS
- Use limeade instead of lemonade.
- Vary the berries: try raspberries or blueberries.
- For a subtle spiciness, add some ginger beer, to taste.

TIPS
- If you don't have soda water, simply use sparkling water or tonic water.
- Garnish with some sliced strawberries.

SPICY HOT CHOCOLATE
WITH ROASTED MARSHMALLOWS

Everybody loves this warming hot chocolate, especially children.
It's so easy to make and a very soothing drink for the end of the day.

SERVES 2

2 TBSP (30 ML) UNSWEETENED COCOA
   POWDER, DIVIDED

1½ CUPS (375 ML) MILK (DAIRY OR DAIRY-
   FREE)

BROWN SUGAR, TO TASTE

½ TSP (2.5 ML) GROUND CINNAMON, DIVIDED

A PINCH OF GROUND NUTMEG

A PINCH OF CAYENNE

MARSHMALLOWS, FOR TOASTING

1. Put a tablespoon of cocoa powder in each of two mugs. Set aside.

2. In a pan over a campfire or on a stove top, heat the milk just until small bubbles form around the edge of the pan (be careful not to boil the milk). Divide the hot milk evenly between the mugs. Stir well.

3. Sweeten each serving with sugar, to taste, and stir in ¼ tsp (1 mL) cinnamon, nutmeg, and cayenne.

4. Toast some marshmallows on a toasting fork or skewer over the fire or using a gas flame on a stove. Pile the marshmallows on top of the spicy cocoa and enjoy.

VARIATIONS

- For a more decadent drink, use drinking chocolate instead of unsweetened cocoa powder.
- To make it a mocha, add some strong instant coffee powder (about 1 tsp/ 5 mL or to taste) to the cocoa.
- Top with whipped cream instead of marshmallows.
- Stir in a pinch of ground cardamom or a splash of vanilla.

REASONS TO CELEBRATE

MAY

There are plenty of reasons to raise a glass in the fifth month of the year. May is Lettuce Month, National Barbecue Month, and Zombie Awareness Month. May is also home to Beer Pong Day (first Saturday), Mother's Day (second Sunday), National Caesar Day (third Thursday), and World Otter Day (last Wednesday).

1. National Purebred Dog Day
2. Brothers and Sisters Day
3. National Paranormal Day
4. Star Wars Day (May the Fourth Be With You!)
5. National No Pants Day
6. Free Comic Book Day
7. National Lemonade Day
8. World Donkey Day
9. National Sleepover Day
10. National Root Canal Appreciation Day
11. National Twilight Zone Day
12. National Limerick Day
13. Top Gun Day
14. Online Romance Day
15. National Chocolate Chip Day
16. National Barbecue Day
17. Pinot Grigio Day
18. Mother Whistler Day
19. National May Ray Day
20. National High Heels Day
21. National Talk Like Yoda Day
22. National Craft Distillery Day
23. World Turtle Day
24. Tiara Day
25. Geek Pride Day
26. National Paper Airplane Day
27. National Melissa Day
28. National Hamburger Day
29. National Golf Day
30. National Water a Flower Day
31. National Macaroon Day

JUNE

June usually marks the end of the school year and the unofficial start to the summer. It's also National Candy Month, Pride Month, and National Great Outdoors Month. Other days to celebrate include National Doughnut Day (first Friday), National Black Bear Day (first Saturday), World Martini Day (third Saturday), and Father's Day (third Sunday).

1. National Go Barefoot Day
2. National Bubba Day
3. National Repeat Day
4. National Cheese Day
5. National Moonshine Day
6. National Drive-In Movie Day
7. National Chocolate Ice Cream Day
8. National Best Friends Day
9. National Donald Duck Day
10. National Eggroll Day
11. National Corn on the Cob Day
12. National Peanut Butter Cookie Day
13. International Axe Throwing Day
14. National Bourbon Day
15. National Megalodon Day
16. National Bloomsday
17. Global Garbage Man Day
18. National Go Fishing Day
19. National Garfield the Cat Day
20. National Vanilla Milkshake Day
21. World Giraffe Day
22. National Onion Rings Day
23. National Pink Day
24. Saint-Jean-Baptiste Day
25. National Leon Day
26. National Canoe Day
27. National Sunglasses Day
28. National Ceviche Day
29. National Waffle Iron Day
30. National Meteor Watch Day

HAPPY HOUR

JULY

A month of longer days and long weekends, July is National Watermelon Month and the start of National Fishing Month. You can also celebrate Lake Superior Day (third Sunday) and National Chili Dog Day (last Thursday). And July is Dog House Repair Month.

1. Canada Day
2. World UFO Day
3. American Redneck Day
4. Independence Day (US)
5. National Ian Day
6. National Fried Chicken Day
7. National Dive Bar Day
8. National Blueberry Day
9. Nunavut Day
10. Don't Step on a Bee Day
11. National Mojito Day
12. Etch-A-Sketch Day
13. International Rock Day
14. National Mac and Cheese Day
15. National Donna Day
16. World Snake Day
17. National Tattoo Day
18. Nelson Mandela International Day
19. National Daiquiri Day
20. National Moon Day
21. Take a Monkey to Lunch Day
22. Spoonerism Day
23. International Yada Yada Yada Day
24. International Tequila Day
25. National Hot Fudge Sundae Day
26. World Tofu Day
27. National Walk on Stilts Day
28. National Waterpark Day
29. National Chicken Wing Day
30. Paperback Book Day
31. Harry Potter's Birthday

AUGUST

August sees cooler nights and usually fewer bugs—you can raise a glass to Psychic Day (first Sunday), New Brunswick Day (first Monday), Regatta Day (first Wednesday), International IPA Day (first Thursday), and International Geocaching Day (third Saturday).

1. Dogust 1st: Universal Birthday for Shelter Dogs
2. National Ice Cream Sandwich Day
3. National IPA Day
4. National Chocolate Chip Cookie Day
5. National Oyster Day
6. National Root Beer Float Day
7. Natal Day
8. International Cat Day
9. Start of Elvis Week
10. World Lion Day
11. Mountain Day
12. World Elephant Day
13. International Lefthanders Day
14. National Creamsicle Day
15. National Acadian Day
16. National Roller Coaster Day
17. National Thrift Shop Day
18. Pinot Noir Day
19. National Soft Ice Cream Day
20. National Bacon Lovers Day
21. Poet's Day
22. National Eat a Peach Day
23. Buttered Corn Day
24. Pluto Demoted Day
25. National Whiskey Sour Day
26. National Toilet Paper Day
27. International Bat Night
28. National Red Wine Day
29. According to Hoyle Day
30. Slinky Day
31. National Trail Mix Day

SEPTEMBER

September marks the unofficial end to summer and the arrival of back-to-school. Home to Batman Day (third Saturday) and National Ghost Hunting Day (last Saturday), it's also National Bourbon Heritage Month, National Velociraptor Awareness Month, and Bear Necessities Month.

1. Alberta Heritage Day
2. World Beard Day
3. National Doodle Day
4. National Wildlife Day
5. World Samosa Day
6. National Coffee Ice Cream Day
7. National Salami Day
8. Star Trek Day
9. International Sudoku Day
10. National TV Dinner Day
11. National Make Your Bed Day
12. National Video Games Day
13. Roald Dahl Day
14. Gobstopper Day
15. National Linguine Day
16. World Barber Day
17. National Cheeseburger Day
18. Rice Krispies Treat Day
19. Talk Like a Pirate Day
20. National Pepperoni Pizza Day
21. World Mini Golf Day
22. Hobbit Day
23. National Checkers Day
24. World Bollywood Day
25. National One-Hit Wonder Day
26. National Alpaca Day
27. World Tourism Day
28. World Maritime Day
29. National Coffee Day
30. Rumi Day

OCTOBER

October is usually the time to pull up the docks and close the cottage.
While you're celebrating the end of another cottage season, you can also toast
Bat Appreciation Month, National Apple Month, Squirrel Awareness Month,
World Smile Day (first Friday), Thanksgiving (second Monday),
and World Lemur Day (last Friday).

1. International Raccoon Appreciation Day
2. National Michelle Day
3. Mean Girls Day
4. National Vodka Day
5. National Kiss a Wrestler Day
6. National Garlic Lovers Day
7. National Bathtub Day
8. World Octopus Day
9. National Mouldy Cheese Day
10. World Porridge Day
11. Southern Food Heritage Day
12. National Pulled Pork Day
13. World Egg Day
14. National Ryan Day
15. National Grouch Day
16. National Dictionary Day
17. Farmers Day
18. National Meatloaf Appreciation Day
19. International Gin and Tonic Day
20. World CRISPR Day
21. International Day of the Nacho
22. Eat a Pretzel Day
23. TV Talk Show Host Day
24. National Bologna Day
25. World Pasta Day
26. Worldwide Howl at the Moon Night
27. Sylvia Plath Day
28. National Chocolate Day
29. National Hermit Day
30. National Candy Corn Day
31. Halloween

"HEY, I SWEAR THERE WERE
CHIPS LEFT IN HERE."
—Suspicious and Snacky

Campfire Stories

DRINK YOUR LAWN CARES AWAY

It's rare for police to charge people with impaired driving of a lawn mower, but if the drunk driver is causing a problem, they have that option.

In the summer of 2020, in the town of Ear Falls, in Northern Ontario, not far from the Manitoba border, a forty-eight-year-old man was suspected of drunk driving of a lawn mower. The main clue to his state was that he was driving the mower down the main street, although he did occasionally veer off to randomly cut—or cut across—the lawns of the town's residents.

CTV News reported that the Ontario Provincial Police found him, arrested him, and tested his blood alcohol levels.

In Canada, not everyone realizes that the crime of impaired driving applies not only to operating cars, but also to boats (including kayaks and canoes), planes, Jet Skis, snowmobiles, and, yes, ride-on lawn mowers. It doesn't matter whether you're driving on a public road or on your own property.

It's rare for police to charge people with impaired driving of a lawn mower, but if the drunk driver is causing a problem, they have that option.

This driver had been causing a commotion and was over the limit. He was charged with operation while impaired, *and* operation while impaired with a blood alcohol concentration over eighty (that's more than eighty milligrams of alcohol per hundred milliliters of blood).

There have been similar cases in Canada. In 2016, the *Sudbury Star* reported a drunk-mowing arrest near the city of Niagara Falls, Ontario. Thirty-four-year old "Willis" was sitting on his ride-on mower with a case of beer between his knees. He drove the mower into a ditch, where a neighbour tried to help him. Police arrived on the scene and found him displaying "extreme signs of impairment." When they took Breathalyzer samples, he was over four times the limit. The case went to court, and Willis received a $2,000 fine and was prohibited from driving for a year.

Drunken mower drivers: they fought the lawn and the law won.

THE BLUE GHOST

Although the tunnel was entirely empty,
it felt as if it was full of activity.

Some years ago, an amateur ghost hunter went off in search of the Screaming Tunnel in the Niagara area. The directions he was given weren't very good and he couldn't find the tunnel he wanted, but he eventually stumbled onto another tunnel, near Thorold, running under what was once part of the Welland Canal.

He snapped some photos of the site using a film camera. Later, when the photos were developed, they showed something strange. There was a figure by the tunnel's entrance—a figure made of blue mist, floating above the ground. He named the place the Blue Ghost Tunnel, and the name has stuck.

The ghost hunter returned with his friends. Some agreed to venture deeper into the blackness of the tunnel. It was an eerie place, the air cool and damp. Aging wooden beams, bound together with rusty steel plates, supported the decaying arch of stones overhead. The tunnel's curved roof echoed back their own footsteps and the constant sound of dripping water.

The explorers could feel a growing tension. Although the tunnel was entirely empty, it felt as if it was full of activity. They seemed to see movements in the periphery of their vision, yet when they turned to look, there was nothing.

Then there were the sounds—they heard the dripping water and their echoing footsteps, but they heard another sound too—something moving around in the darkness. They boldly tried to follow the sound, shining their lights in the direction of the noise. They saw only old stones streaked with minerals and green slime. There was nothing else there—at least nothing living.

As they ventured further in, the light from the tunnel's arched entrance faded, until it was no longer visible at all. The floor became wetter. Soon their boots were sinking into mud, then splashing through water.

Beyond, the tunnel was submerged.

When they were walking back, they heard a loud bang, then saw a floating blue mist, hovering by the entrance. One shocked witness described it as a figure with many faces. It hovered for a time, then vanished.

Others have visited the site, and they also say they have seen strange mists and other phenomena. Some have seen the figure of a child. Some have seen floating lights. One described an orange light speeding down the tunnel.

The mist might be explained away as some kind of vapour, or the breath of the visitors caught in the gleam of their flashlights. But people often comment on that undeniable sense of invisible activity around them, movement and footsteps other than their own.

One visitor said she had been deep in the tunnel when she heard something approaching. She shone her light around but nothing was visible. Still, the feeling grew, and the sound grew louder. With horror she felt something brush past her. Whatever it was didn't stop, continuing into the gloom.

A local man recalled how, as teenagers in the 1970s, he and a group of friends had walked deep into the tunnel. As they reached the submerged area, he felt a sudden sense of deep unease. A coldness descended on them. Ahead, in the flooded darkness, they saw a woman, dressed entirely in black. The teens screamed and ran in terror back to the entrance, slipping and scrambling on the wet floor. They emerged from the tunnel panting and covered in mud. None felt any desire to return.

These are some of the reports we've heard. But what is this tunnel? Is there a history that could explain the unusually varied experiences people have had there?

The Blue Ghost Tunnel was built in the 1870s. Back then, Canada was hard at work building railways and canals to connect the country. The Welland Canal was one of these Victorian megaprojects. In its day, it was considered one of the world's modern wonders, connecting two of the Great Lakes—Lake Ontario and Lake Erie—via a series of locks. The canal had already gone through two incarnations, and in the 1870s and 1880s, engineers created a third version, bigger and straighter.

The canal intersected another great megaproject—the Grand Trunk Railway. In order for the railway to cross the canal at Thorold, engineers dug a long railway tunnel under the waterway. It was named the Merritton Tunnel, honouring William Merritt, who had spearheaded the building of the Welland Canal.

Both the canal and railway are disused now. Since those days, a fourth Welland Canal was built along a different route—it's the canal that ships still use today—and the third canal and the locks running over the Merritton Tunnel have fallen into disrepair.

In recent years, the spooky fame of the tunnel has grown. The owners of the canal land became concerned about people getting hurt in the decaying structure. They have sealed up the entrance, and those who try to get in are stopped by security patrols.

But what about the ghosts? Is there any explanation offered for what people have seen?

There have been some deaths there, certainly. In 1903, two trains collided near the tunnel's entrance. The train engineers survived with minor injuries, but the trains' respective firemen, the men stoking coal into the engines, were not so lucky. As the trains collided, both were thrown towards the flames and the searing boiler. One was terribly burned and died hours later in hospital. The other died at the scene, jammed into the boiler in a state reporters of the day described as "badly mangled." His remains were taken away in pieces.

A train crash might explain the ghostly orange light seen in the tunnel, but what about the other phantoms? The cold blue mist and the variety of faces by the water?

Perhaps there is another possibility.

Not far from the tunnel was an old cemetery, dating back to the late 1700s. Its church was relocated long ago, and the cemetery became neglected and overgrown. Fences broke and cattle wandered over the gravestones to graze. Locals viewed it as an eyesore, an embarrassment to the town of Thorold. They anticipated tourists coming to gaze at the great Welland Canal, one of the engineering marvels of the age. What would those tourists think of Thorold when they glanced in the direction of this run-down, dilapidated old cemetery?

Something had to be done, said the city planners, and finally, in the 1920s, something was done. It was decided that the entire cemetery area should be flooded. It would be turned into a pond to absorb excess water flow. As for the graves on the site, officials promised they would be moved to a larger, more modern cemetery.

The town allowed only a year to move the remains. Family members of the dead paid the costs, but the transfer of so many bodies seems to have been a careless, chaotic process. Monuments were broken. Remains were moved to the wrong grave. Other graves contained only partial remains. It was a mad scramble to complete the work before the water came flooding in, submerging the old cemetery.

Those who have looked at the records spotted a disturbing discrepancy. Although more than 250 graves had been moved, the old church documents show these were just a fraction of the graves in the cemetery. In fact, well over eight hundred people had been buried at the original site.

Perhaps the mysterious blue mists in that cold, wet tunnel are not the ghost of one person but the ghosts of many—restless spirits of those submerged, forgotten souls, trying to leave their cold, flooded graves.

CAMPFIRE STORIES

THE MILKY WAY

Somewhere in the centre of that glowing sphere is one of the most extraordinary objects in the galaxy—a supermassive black hole.

You know you're deep in cottage country when you can see the Milky Way at night. Away from the bright lights of town, with all its buildings, cars, and highways, the night sky becomes much darker. As we stare into the blackness and our eyes adjust to the dark, fainter stars that are unseen in the city and suburbs become visible. And there, stretching across the inky black sky, you will see the great pale glow of the Milky Way.

The name is ancient. In Greek myth, the Milky Way was milk from the breast of the goddess Hera, the wife of Zeus. According to one legend, Zeus had had a fling with a mortal woman, who had a son. Zeus wanted the boy to have godlike powers, which meant he had to suckle from a goddess. When Zeus's wife Hera was asleep, Zeus put the baby Heracles on her breast so the infant could feed. Surprisingly, she slept through this, but when she finally woke up and found a strange baby attached to her, she pushed it away, and a jet of milk sprayed across the sky, producing the Milky Way. The Greek word for "milky" is *galaxias*, so the same legend also gives us our word *galaxy*.

Of course, it's not really milky at all. What appears smooth is actually billions of stars, so far away that they are impossible to see individually. They combine to make a single white blur.

You might wonder why the Milky Way is so difficult to see. You would think all those stars, grouped together, should combine to form something very bright. Why is it that, to see it at all, we need to get far away from any light pollution, and then let our eyes get used to the darkness?

The answer is that the Milky Way has some pollution of its own. This river of milk is far from clean. In fact, when we look at it, we see only the dim glow of light that has managed to reach us through a vast expanse of dirt and dust.

And although milk is high in calcium, a lot of this dust is made of black carbon, so maybe a better name for the Milky Way might be the Sooty Way.

The shroud of dust means that, although we know what distant galaxies look like, the shape of our own has long been a mystery—it's too dirty to see through it, and you'd need to travel an awfully long way to get a top-down view. The images you see of our galaxy in photographs are usually artists' impressions or photographs of a giant neighbour, the Andromeda Galaxy, which is a vast spiral. It used to be thought our galaxy looked similar, but astronomers now believe our galaxy is more like a spiral with a bar in the centre. Both galaxies are on a collision course, and in a few billion years they will merge.

If you could take a galactic broom and sweep all that dust away, the night sky would look very different. The Milky Way would appear as a thick, bright line across the sky, and the bulge in its centre, where a vast number of stars swirl around its core, would shine more brightly than the full moon.

Somewhere in the centre of that glowing sphere is one of the most extraordinary objects in the galaxy—a supermassive black hole.

How massive is supermassive? Well, let's say you start with our solar system—the sun and all its planets. Then you take

four million more solar systems just like it. Squeeze them together into a tight, round ball, and that's how much mass is in that black hole. The gravity at its surface is so intense that the movement of light is frozen and time comes to a stop. Objects don't often collide with the black hole, but huge stars in the grip of its tremendous gravitational pull swoop around it, orbiting it like tiny moons.

Things get even stranger on the outside of the galaxy's swirling disc. Scientists believe it is surrounded by a halo of material known as "dark matter." Nobody knows what it is, but it is completely invisible, and there's a lot of it. In fact, all the things we can see—the stars, planets, dust, and even the black holes—are just a small part of the galaxy's mass. More than 80 percent of the Milky Way is dark matter.

Our galaxy is very old—it formed soon after the Big Bang and has been swirling around ever since, occasionally gobbling up smaller galaxies nearby. We're swirling around with it, of course, but it's a long trip. The journey around the galaxy, a galactic year, takes about 230 million years.

Until the 1920s, many scientists believed our galaxy was the whole universe, a vast collection of countless stars. They looked through their telescopes and saw little clouds and spirals scattered among the stars, but they figured these objects were swirling pools of gas inside our galaxy, perhaps young solar systems forming. Only later did they discover that these smudges and swirls were actually distant collections of stars. At first, they called them "island universes." Now we call them all galaxies, and we've expanded our definition of *universe* to encompass them all. There are a hundred billion stars in our galaxy, but more than two trillion galaxies in the universe.

If those numbers are hard to get your head around, well, don't worry about it. The universe will wait. Go outside and just enjoy looking at the Milky Way. In Canada, it is easiest to see in the summer, when it's in the south. When we see it, we're looking "inward" in the direction of our galaxy's core, which appears as a slight bulge. There's your second full moon, if we could just clean it up a bit.

In winter, we can still see the Milky Way in the heavens, but now we have moved around the sun and face the other way. The milky line is paler and thinner—we're looking out towards the rim of our galaxy, through a wall of invisible dark matter, and gazing out at the universe beyond.

ICE RESCUES

Using hammers and chainsaws, they cut a route through the ice.

Falling through a hole in the ice has long been a risk for Canadians in winter. Experts say the risk is increasing as temperatures get warmer and ice melts earlier than people expect. So it's good to know there are people on hand to rescue others.

Sometimes, though, an attempted rescue can cause problems of its own.

In 2017, a middle-aged couple in Northwestern Ontario took a morning walk on Sandy Lake. It was April. The weather was warming and the ice was melting fast, but it was still thick near the shore.

The woman noticed a dog venturing out towards the centre of the lake. She worried that the ice might break. Her fears were justified. As she watched, the ice cracked beneath its feet and the dog fell into the cold water. It scrambled to get out but was unable to get a grip on the ice around it. Its efforts only broke off more ice. The poor animal was yelping pitifully.

The woman couldn't just watch—she knew she had to help. As her husband looked on and offered advice, she walked carefully across the ice, away from the shore. Unfortunately, ice that is too weak to support a dog will certainly not support a human. She was only partway to the dog when the ice gave way beneath her too, and she found herself up to her neck in near-freezing water.

Alarmed, the husband rushed to help her. Because he was bigger and heavier than she was, he went through the ice even sooner.

Fortunately, a local had witnessed the scene and called the fire department. When emergency workers arrived, they found man, woman, and dog still in their own holes in the ice, each unable to get out. The rescuers put on life jackets and used a kayak to rescue all three from the water.

After half an hour in the water they were very cold, but they all recovered well.

❦ ❦ ❦

It's not just dogs and humans who fall through ice. It can be just as much of a trap for wild animals.

In March 2022, a hunter named Marty Thomas heard that a deer had fallen through ice on the Kettle River in British Columbia. A group of bystanders were trying to help the animal, but nobody could rescue it from the river.

Although he was a hunter, Marty couldn't stand seeing the animal suffer. He tried walking out to the deer, but the ice looked dangerously thin, so he went back and brought a canoe to the scene. He was able to wrap a rope around the deer, then tow it in with the canoe.

The deer was weak from the cold, so Marty carried it back to his truck and took it home. He set up a place for it in a heated cabin, with hay and a blanket. It seemed to work, because when he checked back later, the animal had left.

In 2022, a group of loggers working in northwestern Ontario managed an even more spectacular ice rescue. A cow moose had fallen through the ice on Windigoostigwan Lake. Usually, a moose can work its way out of ice, but this animal had been struggling for hours, sometimes putting its head on the ice to rest. Left to its own devices, it was surely doomed.

The men figured that, if they could cut a channel in the ice, they could guide the moose to a shallower area of the river. If the moose's feet could reach the bottom, it might have a chance of getting itself out. A moose is a powerful animal, and they knew the rescue was potentially dangerous.

Using hammers and chainsaws, they cut a route through the ice. The moose watched them apprehensively, then swam closer to the shallower water.

Eventually the loggers cut a path to an area where the water was only a few feet deep. Finally the moose was able to clamber out onto the ice. The loggers drew back and gave it some space. After a few minutes recovering its strength, the moose got to its feet, gave one last look at the loggers, and loped off into the forest.

* * *

If you or your pets really must fall through the ice, it pays to do so in just the right place.

A woman in Hay River, in the Northwest Territories, owned two Great Danes. The dogs ventured out onto the river as temperatures were rising. Both dogs fell through the ice.

The owner was beside herself and didn't know what to do—she knew that trying to reach them could be dangerous.

Fortunately, she lived near a Canadian Coast Guard base. Three men from the base spotted the dogs, sized up the situation, and moved into action, strapping on their life jackets and putting an aluminum boat into the water. The rescue took about fifteen minutes. As the dogs came out of the water, they were shaking and bruised but alive. The owner was astonished . . . and deeply grateful.

* * *

A coordinated group effort by amateurs can save a life when people move fast enough.

In January 2014, a group of friends were snowshoeing in Cape Breton. They were visiting a popular local site, Uisge Ban Falls near Baddeck. In winter, the falls form spectacular icicles.

According to CBC News, one man, Julien Rouleau, was exploring the area, not realizing how close he was to the edge of the falls. The snow and ice below him gave way and he fell, sliding down the ice as if he were on a waterslide, then disappearing into the ice-covered pool at the bottom.

Julien fell to the bottom of the pool and found himself unable to get back up—the cold water from the waterfall was keeping him under.

Luckily his friends had seen him plunge through the ice. When he didn't come up again, they hurried down to help. They formed a human chain, and the person at the front placed a ski pole into the pond.

When they felt their friend grab it under the water, they pulled him to the surface.

Rouleau was deeply affected by the experience. He said you don't realize how precious life is until you almost have it taken away from you.

THE GHOST SONG

She noticed patches of flattened grass, slowly regaining their shape.
Something had been by there, and fairly recently.

The following story was told to us by a woman we'll call "Sarah." Some years ago, she was working in the Yukon as a nature interpreter. She was at ease in the northern forest and wanted to learn more about the animals and walk the trails made by the moose and bears. She set off on a five-day solo hike in an area now known as Tombstone Territorial Park, north of Dawson.

The region is just 160 kilometres from the Arctic Circle. It is named for Tombstone Mountain, whose peaks were thought to resemble a graveyard against the northern sky.

Sarah drove to the park along the Dempster Highway. The two-lane gravel road follows the old dogsled route from Dawson City to Fort McPherson and provides the only road entrance to the park.

She left the car, and civilization, behind. She had the company of her faithful husky, the aging leader of her dog team, a veteran of many nights sleeping curled up beneath the starry winter skies. She carried a big backpack and a sturdy walking staff. She found her own path, balancing on rocks across the river, picking up a faint game trail in the thick willow bush, using her senses to tell her where the surest footing would be found, where a broader trail would be: Where do the animals like to walk? How does the land lie?

After two days of hiking, she had climbed out of the familiar valley and dropped over a saddle of high ground into new territory. Unknown, untravelled, filled with the scent of forest and the promise of discovery.

She was in the midst of true northern wilderness now, subarctic alpine landscapes, where rivers tumble through rock and lichen, and sharp mountain peaks glower from above.

It was late summer. Squirrels chattered in the spruce trees, gathering cones. Blueberries ripened on the mountain slopes. The valleys lay warm in the afternoon sun.

Sarah followed a game trail, using her map and compass to check her bearings each time she left one valley and struck down another. She hiked up a steep slope to the saddleback that would take her to the next part of her journey.

Along the way, she saw an animal loping along. It was a little smaller than her dog, but powerfully built. She recognized it as a wolverine, a notoriously cautious animal that rarely comes within sight of humans. The wolverine passed her, then crawled behind a boulder, baring its formidable teeth and hissing.

Further up the slope, she found a pool surrounded by soft, bright-green grass—a dramatic contrast to the plants struggling in the rocky land around her. Sarah thought of pausing for a rest and a drink of water after her steep ascent under the afternoon sun. Then she noticed patches of flattened grass, slowly regaining their shape. Something had been by there, and fairly recently. Was it the wolverine she had seen hours earlier? She looked more closely and found clearer tracks—she was no hunter, but those were definitely bear tracks. In these parts, that almost certainly meant a grizzly. Maybe it would be better to press on. She kept going, keeping her eyes open and her dog close.

Soon she reached a new valley. It had looked accessible on the map, but in reality the path down was a treacherous slope strewn with huge, sharp boulders. The dog was reluctant to go, so she had to urge and then carry the frightened animal, going in stages from boulder to boulder, first taking the backpack, then returning for the twenty-five-kilogram dog. She finally reached the bottom. It had been an exhausting descent, and she hoped the path ahead would be easier.

It certainly was. A streamside trail led her into a beautiful valley, where grass and lichen were growing alongside little thickets of willow. A stream braided its waters over the smooth cobbles.

High up on the mountainside, a group of Dall sheep grazed on a grassy slope. They are Yukon's distinctive wild sheep with white fur and large curved horns.

Sarah knew something about the history of this region. It was the land of the Gwich'in, one of the most northerly of the Indigenous Peoples, who live in the Arctic community of Old Crow. Long ago, the Gwich'in had often fished and hunted in this area, and this valley, surely, must have been one of their haunts.

The afternoon was drawing on, and clouds were starting to gather. She felt a few drops of rain. It was time to make camp quickly, get the tent up, and put some firewood under the shelter of the fly before everything was soaked. She thought she would set up a tent near one of the willow thickets. These willows are stunted little growths—more bush than tree—but in the centre of the thicket it's easy to find deadwood that can be pulled out and used to make a campfire.

Sarah prepared to set up her camp. But she had hardly begun when she thought she heard a sound—human voices. She looked around, wondering if it was a hunting party, but there was no sign of other people. Perhaps she had misheard.

Then the sound came again—yes, it was unmistakably a group of voices, people conversing. There must be campers around. But where was their camp?

She listened more attentively now. A fitful wind was blowing, and the voices came and went on the breeze. It was strange: she could hear the voices well enough, and they had to be coming from somewhere in the valley, yet there didn't seem to be anyone else there. She wondered if she had imagined it. But there! The sounds came again—a group of voices. Women, she now thought. And as she kept straining her ears, she heard the talking change to singing—Sarah could hear fragments of the music. She couldn't make out the tune or the words, but she could hear they were enjoying themselves, women singing in different registers.

She checked up and down. She pulled the binoculars from her backpack

and scanned the area. There were no tents. No fires. She saw other willow thickets but nobody was camped in them or beyond them. This might be a perfect place to camp—there was no place for a noisy group of campers to hide out of sight.

She could tell the general direction the sounds were coming from—they seemed to be only a few hundred metres away. She considered walking in the direction of the sounds. Perhaps following the singing would reveal an answer.

But something about this idea made her deeply uncomfortable. Sarah could cope with grizzly bears and wolverines, but this singing had her feeling spooked, and the longer she listened to those faceless voices, the more spooked she became.

Instead, she packed up her backpack and left the area. The singing faded behind her as she walked away, and when the voices were out of earshot, she felt nothing but relief. She would camp further along, where the environment was more ordinary—more natural and less supernatural.

Looking back at the event, Sarah is at a loss to explain what she heard that day. She has read about research into the acoustic properties of trees. Apparently some tree species reflect sound in different ways than others. Could these reflected sounds somehow be the explanation for the half-heard conversations and singing—was it some sort of acoustic illusion? Perhaps.

But Sarah wonders, too, about *another* possibility. A few years after her hike, she heard of a legend told by some Indigenous Peoples in Canada's north. It is said that when a group makes a camp among the trees and they sing together, some of the music is caught in the branches. It's also said that when you go to the places where people camped centuries before, you can still hear the echoes of those long-ago voices—the singing of the ancestors.

THE NIAGARA SCOW

The two men realized with horror that they
were being swept down towards the falls.

Niagara Falls is one of the world's great natural wonders. Although it is surrounded by industry and tourist shops, nothing can detract from the awesome power of the falls, more than two million litres of water pouring over the precipice every second. As you look down on it, you can't help but think on what a terrible thing it would be to fall in, or to be in a boat without power, careening towards that deadly drop.

It has happened for real, many times. One of these events is described in T.W. Kriner's book *In the Mad Water: Two Centuries of Adventure and Lunacy at Niagara Falls*, which recounts many strange events.

In 1918 two deckhands were working on a scow, or dumping barge, owned by the Great Lakes Dredge and Docks Company. One man was more experienced. He was Gustave Lofberg, a fifty-one-year-old Swede who had spent many years work-

ing on and around the Great Lakes. His assistant was James Harris, forty. Harris was a newcomer to this work—he'd been doing it for only a month. It paid the bills to support his wife and five children. Both men lived in Buffalo, New York.

The scow was a flat-bottomed rectangular barge. The vessel and its two crew members were part of an unglamorous operation to remove sand and silt from the bottom of a canal on the American side owned by Hydraulic Power Company of Niagara Falls, based in Niagara Falls, New York. Crews on dredging platforms scooped up sand and silt and muck from the bottom, then dumped it into the metal scows. A number of tugboats pulled the scows from place to place, towing them away when they were full.

The tug pulling their scow, which carried two thousand tons of silt, was the *Hassayampa*. Three long steel cables connected the barge to the tug and allowed the powerful ship to haul the heavy scow through the fast waters of the Niagara River. On that day, though, the tug had run into a problem. It had run aground on a sandbar. The tug was tipped to one side and unable to get itself free. Fortunately, there were four other tugs in the area, and they moved in to shift the grounded vessel.

Two of the tugs, *Mayer* and *Kinch*, moved alongside the *Hassayampa*, and with a sudden jolt, the tug was free. In the same instant, the steel cables snapped like string.

Harris and Lofberg were doing their work on the scow and didn't realize anything was wrong at first. Then they noticed they were moving, and they were getting further from their tug as they drifted to the Canadian side of the river and downstream. At the same moment, a chorus of whistles from the tugboat fleet raised an alarm. The two men realized with horror that they were being swept down towards the falls.

Lofberg knew they had to act fast. The scow had an anchor—a six-ton block of concrete. Lofberg and Harris released it, sending the massive block to the bottom of the river. But the six-ton weight was no match for the momentum of the barge's enormous load. The barge slowed a little, but it kept moving on down the river, dragging its anchor behind it.

As the men sped past the rapids and looked ahead at the rising mist of the falls,

it seemed certain they were about to face the nightmare plunge over the edge. The drop was less than a kilometre away and coming up fast. If they jumped from the barge, they would be unable to outswim the current. They had only minutes to live.

At that moment, a great grinding sound came from below them. The scow had scraped to a halt on the rocks below. The vessel was still swaying, though, and it might easily work free again. The two deckhands created another impromptu anchor, fastening a cable to a piece of heavy hardware, and threw it over the side. Lofberg then started opening the barge's watertight compartments, flooding the vessel. The flat-bottomed barge was already resting on the rock, but he reasoned that, if they could make it sink, the vessel would rest more firmly on the rocks below them.

The barge seemed to settle, although it still swayed with the current. But how were they going to get back to shore? The rapids and the torrent of the Niagara River lay between them and the land.

In the meantime, news of the accident had spread fast. Huge crowds gathered by the river to see the scow and its unfortunate crew. Authorities on both sides of the border were scrambling to figure out a rescue plan.

The first attempt involved using a rescue cannon—a small cannon that fires a lifeline with a grappling hook. But the cannon wasn't powerful enough for the job, and a groan went up from the crowd as the line fell into the water.

Attempts were made to float a row of wooden platforms down the river. This, too, was a failure.

More equipment arrived on the scene—a bigger rescue cannon. It took an hour to set up the equipment. The operators took careful aim and fired. The rope arced over the barge and landed across it. Harris and Lofberg grabbed the wet rope and fastened it to a winch. This light rope would not carry the weight of the men, but it would let the rescuers send a second, heavier rope. For the next three hours, the two men on the barge and the rescuers on the shore worked to drag a second line to the barge. By the time they were done, it was getting dark. Fortunately, one thing Niagara Falls had in abundance was electricity. A group of massive searchlights was trained on the scow.

The plan was to rescue the marooned crew using a breeches buoy—a combination of a zip line and a floating life ring. In the centre of the ring is a pair of fabric "breeches." The person to be rescued places their legs in the holes and can be hauled along the guy line above. But using the device was more difficult than it sounds. As the buoy was sent across to the men,

CAMPFIRE STORIES

the line sagged, and the buoy fell into the river. It was swept along on the current and hit a rock, where it became trapped. The two crewmen watched with alarm. If that had happened while they were on the rescue mechanism, they would certainly have died.

The rescue team worked into the night to free the trapped buoy, but without success. A message was sent to the crew, written on giant signs. "Rest." Neither Lofberg nor Harris got much sleep. They were starting to despair of being rescued.

Around three in the morning, one of the workers, a man named William Hill, suggested a daring plan. He volunteered to go down on the rope, riding a second buoy. If he could reach the first buoy, he believed he could untangle the line. The officers in charge accepted the brave offer. Hill made two dangerous descents, first freeing a jammed block, then going back to untangle the line. He succeeded. Two hours later, the rescue line was finally back in place, and the breeches buoy was sent across for the first crew member.

Harris went first. He placed his legs into the buoy. Lofberg told him to pull on the rope above him—it would keep his buoy close to the overhead line as the rescuers pulled him back. Harris was soon on his way, but he was exhausted and lacked the strength to pull on the rope. The line sagged and Harris dipped into the river as he crossed. Although he had a flotation ring around him, he came close to drowning. It took all the team's efforts to bring Harris to land.

Lofberg went next. He was tired too, but he used the last of his strength to haul his buoy up close to the line. Photographs from the day show him being pulled across, high above the water. It was a quick and efficient crossing. The rescue made headlines around the world.

The next day, the two men went back to work.

The old scow did not go over the falls, although the hulk is breaking apart and may soon be swept away. For now, it can still be seen, not far from the falls, rusting away in the river.

RECENT IMMIGRANTS

If you hate pulling dandelions, blame the European settlers.

When we think of invasive species, we think of accidental invaders like zebra mussels and giant hogweed, but many of the non-native plants and animals that have spread across Canada were put here deliberately. When Europeans first moved to North America, people were nostalgic for the old country. Among the things they missed were the plants and birds of their homelands.

Attitudes to ecology were very different in the nineteenth and early twentieth centuries. Americans and Canadians formed "acclimatization societies"—organizations whose goal was to make North America look cozier and more familiar by introducing European species like chaffinches, European robins, blackbirds, and house sparrows. Most didn't take, but the sparrows spread like wildfire across New York and beyond.

One man who was heavily involved in this work was an American pharmacist named Eugene Schieffelin. In 1877, he became president of the American Acclimatization Society. Schieffelin was an eccentric. According to some sources, he had two passions—birds and Shakespeare—and he combined these interests in his quest to take every bird species mentioned by Shakespeare and introduce it to North America.

One of these birds was the starling. Shakespeare name-dropped the starling in *Henry IV*, Part 1, when a character named Hotspur suggests teaching a starling to speak the name of one of the king's enemies, then sending the bird to the king as a gift to annoy him. This plan is not as crazy as it sounds—starlings come from the same family as myna birds and can learn to imitate human speech, just as parrots can.

Schieffelin imported a group of starlings and released them in Central Park around 1890. The birds flourished and their population exploded across the continent. They are now one of the most common birds in Canada—their North American numbers are in the hundreds of millions—and they are accused of displacing many native species.

While the starling may have been an ecological disaster, it remains a fascinating little bird, with its oily black feathers and iridescent "stars." Their flocks can be huge, and the shifting patterns they form as they fly (known as murmurations) are an amazing sight. It's also interesting to hear the sounds of the starling as it imitates other birds. The composer Mozart kept a starling as a pet and was enchanted with the creature's aptitude for copying words and music. When it died after a few years, he gave it an elaborate ceremony.

Canadians have enjoyed starlings in the same way. A girl named Izumi Kyle found an abandoned baby starling in Toronto. Her family raised it and named it Kuro. It became a member of the family, flying around the house and imitating words, music, and the sounds of household appliances. It lived longer than any other known starling—an astonishing nineteen years.

Introduced species weren't only birds. Many of our common plants are also imports. If you hate pulling dandelions, blame the European settlers. They brought the plant to the eastern parts of North America for its use as food and medicine. Now it has spread across Canada—as well as the rest of North America and South America. And don't think you can get away from pulling dandelions by moving to other parts of the world—similar efforts to introduce the dandelion were equally successful in Australia, New Zealand, Africa, and India.

Another alien plant grows along roads and streams. It's the teasel—a tall plant with spiky bulbs at the top of its stems. We're so used to it that it seems a natural part of the landscape, but it too was deliberately introduced to North America— this time by wool workers, who used the dried plant heads to tease out the wool on cloth. Again, the plant has spread widely, growing in dense clumps and crowding out the native plants.

One of the most invasive species in Canada, and one that has made a difference to the look of our wild places, is a creature we might not think twice about— the humble earthworm.

Before Europeans arrived in Canada, there were no earthworms at all across most of the country. They were wiped out millions of years ago by the glaciers. We're often told that earthworms are "good for the soil," aerating it and fertilizing it. The truth is that earthworms are good for some plants and animals and not for others.

Worms eat dead vegetable matter, like leaves that have fallen to the ground. They crawl out of their holes at night, grab a leaf, and pull it under, turning the leaf into soil. But if plants or animals depend on a protective layer of decomposing leaves, the worms are a disaster, because they will remove that layer. The presence of worms also changes the acidity of soil. Plants that flourished in one level of acidity may not do so well in another.

A few centuries ago, most Canadian forests were covered in a thick layer of leaf. Flowers like the trillium flourished in those conditions, and salamanders scampered under the wet leaves, protected from the hot sun and hungry birds. That has all changed.

Worms arrived in Canada quite recently, probably around the mid-1800s. They were not a project of the acclimatization societies. In fact, nobody paid much attention to how they arrived, but they were probably bought by settlers in their plant pots, or in ship ballast that was dumped on land.

But they did arrive, and every time they were dumped in a new patch of soil, they multiplied and moved slowly outward, spreading like bacteria on a culture. Gradually, the forests across Canada took on a different appearance—the leaf litter in the forests disappeared and the ground became bare.

Sometimes the worms get a lift to virgin land—anglers bring them along to do some fishing, then dump their leftover worms on the ground when they're done, not realizing they're seeding a new colony of worm pioneers.

The worms claim their territory slowly but steadily. The range of each worm kingdom expands by about a kilometre every hundred years. Even at that pace, it hasn't taken them long to cover most of the provinces. Only Alberta remains mostly worm-free—although numbers are expanding there too.

We can't remove all these invasive species from Canada. Perhaps it would be hypocritical to try—after all, we're an invasive species ourselves. But we're learning more every day about the complex, interesting ways that different species affect each other. With knowledge and care, we can appreciate the plants and animals that belong here, as well as the ones we've introduced, and perhaps find ways for them to coexist.

CAMPFIRE STORIES

THE COFFIN

The coffin had moved again.

A guy named Mark was out in the woods on a camping trip. But it wasn't going very well. He had started the trip with a cold and hadn't managed to shake it, so he was constantly blowing his nose and taking cough syrup. He tried to start a campfire, but the wood wouldn't light no matter what he did. And when he settled into his tent at night, a heavy rain started. The seams of his tent began leaking, and the rain came pouring in. Sleeping was impossible.

He remembered passing an abandoned cabin on his way into the woods. It was a rickety old place, but it was close by, and Mark figured it had to be better than his leaky tent. So he grabbed his backpack and flashlight and ran for the cabin.

The inside of the cabin surprised him. It was a large place with several rooms, and best of all, it was dry. There was nobody there—just a few boxes piled up. Mark went into one of the rooms and lay down.

He was just falling asleep when he was jolted awake by a noise, like something scraping along the floor. He thought he'd imagined it, but then he heard it again—a noise from near the door. He got up and went out there, shining his flashlight around. The light fell on a big box. No, not a box, he realized. It was a coffin—plain oak. He didn't remember seeing it when he came in, but he figured it had been dark and he had other things on his mind.

Mark went back to his room and tried to sleep.

He heard it again. A noise. Something heavy moving across the floor.

He went out to the hall again. There was nobody there—but the coffin seemed to have moved. He was sure it had been on the far side of the hall, but now it lay across the floor, between Mark and the exit.

"A trick of the light," Mark said to himself. He turned back to his room and had just gone in when he heard a thud. He flashed the light around.

The coffin had moved again. It was now standing upright.

Mark was feeling really scared now. He went into his room and closed the door.

Outside, he heard more noises—the sound of wood grinding against the floor, getting louder and louder. The coffin was coming closer. It seemed like it was right outside the door now.

The sound stopped. Mark sat in the darkness, shining his light around the room in case anything was creeping up.

After a minute or two, he said to himself, "This can't be real. I was probably having a dream. Or it's my cold playing tricks with my head."

He approached the door, put his hand on the handle, turned it, and pulled the door open.

There was the coffin, filling the doorway!

Mark gave a scream and fell back. As he did so, he saw the coffin slide forward. And in the depths of his soul, he knew that coffin had come for him, and he knew too that, if it reached him, he would die.

There was no way out of the room without going past the coffin. Mark cowered in the corner as the coffin kept grinding forward over the wooden floor, coming closer and closer.

He had to stop it. He had his tent mallet with him, and he hurled it at the coffin. It just bounced off. The coffin kept coming closer. It was just three metres away now. Then two metres away . . .

He scrambled in his backpack. He found his hatchet and threw that. The blade stuck in the wood. But no! It had no effect. The coffin kept moving, kept coming closer. Now it was just a metre away.

Mark's fumbling hands felt his bottle of cough syrup. In desperation, he seized the bottle and, with all his strength, hurled it at the coffin. The bottle smashed. The syrup dripped down the wood.

The cough syrup worked. The coffin stopped.

"NO WI-FI, NO NETFLIX, NO PROBLEM."
—UNPLUGGED AND UNWINDING

Games & Jokes

BEER PONG
(OR "ANY DRINK" PONG)
WITH FUN VARIATIONS

Basically, beer pong is a drinking game in which opposing players toss a Ping-Pong ball across a table at a set of partly filled cups arranged on the opposite end. Simply stated, the goal is to land the ball in a cup of beer. It is usually played in teams of two but can also be played one-on-one. Each time a ball lands in a cup, that cup is removed from the table and the defending team takes a drink. Fans may enjoy some options that add a bit of zing to this favourite cottage activity.

By the way, the drinks in this drinking game don't need to be beer—or even alcoholic. Many players prefer water in the cups, and players can have whatever they like in the cup they're actually drinking from. Kids especially are happy with juice or pop and are welcome to play.

Here are some variations on this popular cottage game. Just be sure the rules are agreed on *before* the game begins!

- **TRICK SHOT.** If the ball rolls or bounces back to the shooter and the shooter grabs it before it hits the floor, they can do an extra "trick shot." Ex-

amples: shooting with your eyes closed, from behind your back, from over your shoulder, or off a wall. If the ball sinks, it counts as one cup as usual.

- **GOALIE.** Players can either use a finger or blow in the cup to get the ball out if it's spinning around the inner rim before landing.
- **BONUS.** If both players on a team, or both shots in one turn, land, then that team gets another turn right away. Alternatively, you could have a single bonus shot when both shots land.
- **BOUNCE CON.** If a ball bounces on the table before reaching the cups, the defending team can swipe it away or catch it, ending the throwing team's turn.
- **BOUNCE PRO.** If a bounce shot lands in a cup, it's worth two cups. The defending team picks which second cup to remove. This rule doesn't apply on the final two cups. (Those bounce shots are worth one cup only.)
- **AIR BALL.** When the ball overshoots the table, if the defending team calls "air ball" before the shot has finished, they get the balls back—in other words, the throwing team's turn is over.

- **ISLAND.** Once the game is in play, if there's a cup that is not touching any others—because the surrounding cups have already been hit—a player can call "island" and aim for that cup. If they sink it, it's worth two. If they sink a different cup, though, it's worth nothing. If they sink an isolated cup without calling "island" beforehand, it's just a regular hit.
- **TRIPLE YOUR MONEY.** If both shots in one turn land in the same cup, it's worth three cups. The shooting team can decide which two extra cups are removed. For the final three cups, this shot is worth only two. On the final two cups, it's either worth only one or you can agree in advance whether it takes out the last cup.
- **SHUT OUT.** When one team sinks all their cups before the other team has hit any, the winning team can challenge the opposing team to do something. You can make it anything at all. Perhaps "losing team has to bring us our snacks or drinks for the rest of the night" or "losing team has to perform an interpretive dance to a song of the winning team's choice."
- **FIXING CUPS.** A player can always ask to have the cups they're shooting at fixed, which means returned to their original position. (This would happen if the cups were knocked or slid out of position. This is not the same as re-racking, which is when you ask the other team to rearrange their cups into a new shape. Typically, a team will ask for this when several cups have been removed and the remaining ones are spread out, which makes it harder to hit a cup. There are multiple shape variations, but usually the goal is for the cups to make a compact target. Decide in advance how many re-racks each team gets. A common rule is two per game.)
- **REDEMPTION 1: OVERTIME.** When one team has sunk their last cup, the would-be losing team has a final chance to continue the game. There are a couple of ways to do this. First, they can shoot until they miss—in other words, if they sink all their remaining cups, the game then goes into three-cup overtime, where a triangle of three cups is set up for each team and they continue play as normal.
- **REDEMPTION 2: NOT OVER TILL IT'S OVER.** The would-be losing team gets two or three remaining shots (regardless of the number of cups they have left). If they sink all of them, those cups are removed, the would-be winning team's last cup stays on the table, and gameplay continues.

COTTAGE CHUCKLERS

Knock, knock. Who's there? Philip. Philip who?
Philip the gas tank before we head to the cottage.

What has antlers and sucks blood?
A moose-quito.

How do you keep a skunk from smelling?
Hold its nose.

What do caribou have that no other animal has?
Baby caribou.

What's the difference between a cat and a frog?
A cat has nine lives. A frog croaks every night.

Who lives in Prince Edward Island and bakes funny-coloured bread and rolls?
Anne of Green Bagels.

What's the difference between a mosquito and a fly?
A mosquito can fly, but a fly can't mosquito.

How do grizzlies catch fish?
They use their bear hands.

What do you call bears with no ears?
Bs.

What do you find hanging from maple trees?
You find that your arms get sore.

Why don't they play cards in the jungle?
Too many cheetahs.

What day does a fish hate the most?
Fry-day.

What do you call a bear with no teeth?
A gummy bear.

How do you get a squirrel to be your friend?
Climb a tree and act like a nut.

What books do skunks read?
Best smellers.

What does a duck like to have as a snack?
Milk and quackers.

What do you call a boomerang that doesn't come back?
A stick.

COTTAGE CHARADES

*There's no shortage of good ideas for a game of charades at the cottage.
Here are some possibilities to get you started . . .
inspired by cottage routines and activities.*

Playing croquet

Chopping firewood

Doing a cannonball

Lying in a hammock

Mowing the grass

Paddling a canoe

Pitching a tent

Playing horseshoes

Playing tennis

Playing volleyball

Raking leaves

Roasting a hotdog

Rolling up a sleeping bag

Surfing

Swatting mosquitoes

Sweeping the floor

Taking a cold shower

Throwing a Frisbee

Walking the dog

Waterskiing

RETURN TO THE ROOST

(Half a Ghost Story)

The day was unusual for early November. The weather was bracing, but the sky was a clear, brilliant blue and the lake almost eerily serene. For Dan Perry, it was the best time of the year. Not only was it his birthday month, but this would be a milestone birthday. He'd be turning twenty-five—a quarter of a century. At the same time, the health care start-up he had founded a year earlier was attracting serious investors. Dan was in a mood not so much to celebrate but to reflect. So he had come to his favourite place: his grandfather's cottage. He'd be closing it up, but at the same time, he would be thinking about his future as he marked a new chapter in his life and his career.

The trees were bare and just slightly wet. Dan crunched a carpet of colourful leaves underfoot. He was grateful to be alone with nature. Really alone. The other families on Grey Rock Lake had all closed up a couple of weeks earlier. Their cottages were much more modern affairs than Gramps' cottage, which was, in fact, a modest two-storey wood cabin. Before leaving, Dan would drain the water pipes, and the next week Gramps would arrange for the electricity and landline phone to be discontinued for the winter.

This year, Dan craved solitude. He would be about twenty-five kilometres from the nearest village—more accurately, a hamlet, with a population of about three hundred people. He knew the cell service was sketchy at best, and that pleased him too.

Gramps and Nana had bought "the Roost," as the original cabin was called, when they were newly married and about the age Dan was now. Gramps and Nana spent every summer—and weekends in the spring and autumn months—at the Roost until Nana passed away a couple of years ago. They hadn't planned on buying a property so early in their marriage, but because of a series of circumstances, sad circumstances, they were able to pick it up for an affordable price. Over the years, Dan's parents built their own cottage across the lake.

The original owner, who had built the cabin, was a sculptor, Charles Cornish,

GAMES & JOKES

whose greatest fame came years after his mysterious death. Today, Cornish's works are highly prized and displayed across Canada and internationally, but in the early 1980s he, his wife, Myrna, and their twelve-year-old daughter, Becky, lived in near isolation from early spring to late fall. Then, on a calm early November morning in 1983, Charles and Becky set out on the lake in a sailboat. Myrna had begged them not to venture out, reminding Charles that the lake's calmness could dramatically change. But Becky was eager to have one last sail before returning to the village for the next five months. She pleaded with her father, and Charles could never disappoint his beloved daughter.

To Myrna's relief, the day remained peaceful. And yet, by late afternoon, Charles and Becky hadn't returned. Around 5 p.m., Myrna alerted the police, who would search the lake for two days and then dredge it. Meanwhile, people from the village came together to scour the surrounding woods. But there was never any sign of Charles, or Becky, or the sailboat.

Myrna didn't return to the village that year, desperately hoping her husband and daughter would show up as mysteriously as they had disappeared. Over time, she became reclusive, lost in her memories. Less than two years later, she would die in her sleep—of a broken heart, many said. Family members cleaned out the old cabin and listed it for sale. The

real estate agent explained that because of the stigma associated with the property, they would need to sell it cheap. Gramps and Nana heard about the sale from a friend in the village. While others may have been discouraged by the achingly sad history of the property, they had a different point of view. They could honour the memory of the Cornishes—Charles, Myrna, and Becky—by bringing new life to a beautiful place. That's why Gramps had also purchased Charles Cornish's sculpture of a young girl, said to be inspired by young Becky.

Dan unpacked his car, walked the fifty steps to the cabin, and turned the key in the sturdy wooden door. A blast of cold wind greeted him, and he was surprised to face a wide-open window. "How strange," he thought as he shut it. "So unlike Gramps." He turned up the thermostat but didn't hear the familiar hum that reassuringly indicated the heat had kicked in. Had Gramps forgotten Dan was spending the weekend at the Roost and already had the electricity turned off? Dan went to check the phone. It too was dead.

Dan thought about driving to the village, but it was already late in the afternoon and he didn't want to return to a dark cottage. At least there were candles and a flashlight, plus a kerosene space heater. And, fortunately, Dan had loaded his cooler with some sandwiches and water. He decided to make the most of things and would return to the city the next morning rather than stay the weekend.

With flashlight in hand, Dan headed up the creaky stairs. He opened the door to one of the three bedrooms, the one he had slept in as a young boy. Dusk was approaching, but light still filtered through the window and onto the old carpet. Dan scanned the room—an old chest of drawers, a single bed, an armchair. On the chest was the sculpture of Charles Cornish's young daughter.

Once he had unpacked, Dan went downstairs, the steps creaking. The space heater had by now kicked in, but once again, he was surprised by a sharp blast of wind. He looked up to see the window—the same window he had closed just minutes earlier—wide open again.

Dan Perry was a logical thinker, but he could not come up with a logical explanation. Did he just *think* he had closed the window? Had he told himself he'd close it and then become distracted? That was the best he could come up with, and he wasn't convinced. So he slammed it shut once again, and this time said, out loud, "The window is shut." Then he said, this time to himself, "I am *not* going nuts."

But then, when he went back upstairs and walked into the bedroom—the one with the sculpture of the young girl— something he saw made him stop dead in his tracks. The sculpture was there as it had always been, on the old chest of draw-ers. But now, wrapped around the neck of the girl who was said to be young Becky Cornish was a garland of dried roses.

Dan Perry froze where he stood, unable to move. And what he saw next made his heart beat faster and his entire body tremble with fear.

AT THIS POINT, IT'S UP TO YOU TO FINISH THE STORY. ALL YOU KNOW IS THAT DAN SAW A GHOST . . . OR THE TRICKERY OF A GHOST. BUT WHO IS THIS GHOST? IS HE OR SHE A GOOD GHOST OR A NASTY ONE? AND WHAT DOES OUR GHOST HAVE IN STORE FOR DAN?

GAMES & JOKES

THEMES

*Play with two teams, two to five players
on each team, and a moderator.*

The moderator decides on six themes. Examples: Things That Are Wet, Things That Grow, Things You Do at the Cottage. For each theme, the moderator prepares an index card with five keywords or phrases that describe the theme. Examples of keywords or phrases that describe Things That Are Wet: "swimmers," "a noodle," "a diaper," "chicken soup," "a person in capsized canoe."

To start a round, each team selects a theme and picks a player to be the "caller" (the person who will describe the keywords to their team by giving clues). Callers cannot use the keyword itself, or the theme, in a clue. (Example: For the theme Things That Are Wet and the keyword "swimmers," the caller can't say "swim" or "swimming" or "wet"). Non-verbal clues such as those in pantomime are accepted, e.g., a person acting out front crawl.

The caller gives clues for each keyword, in order, until their team guesses correctly or a time limit for each phrase is reached, and then moves on to the next keyword or phrase. One point is scored for each correct answer. If a caller gives an illegal clue, they must move on to the next keyword or phrase. If a caller decides to skip a keyword, they can go back to it later if they have extra time after their last keyword. At the end of a theme's last keyword or phrase, the other team chooses a theme and the game continues. When all themes have been played, the team with the most points is declared the winner.

PUCKING PUNNY

I think hockey's a great game. Of course, my mom is a dentist.

How do hockey players stay cool?
By sitting next to the fans.

What has twelve legs and goes slurp, slurp?
A hockey team drinking Gatorade.

What does Scrooge wear to play hockey?
Cheap skates.

Why was the centipede kicked off the hockey team?
He took too long to put his skates on.

What do you call a monkey that wins the Stanley Cup?
A chimpion.

What hockey player wears the biggest helmet?
The one with the biggest head.

Why did the hockey player bring string to the game?
So she could tie the score.

What did the skeleton drive to the hockey game?
A Zam-bony.

What did the skate say to the helmet?
You should go on a head while I continue on foot.

What do a magician and a hockey player have in common?
They both do hat tricks.

What hockey player can open any door?
Wayne Gretz-key.

Where do hockey players go when they're in New York City?
The Empire Skate Building.

Did you hear about the guy who went to a fight?
A hockey game broke out.

What position does a monster play on a hockey team?
Ghoulie.

Why can't you play hockey with pigs?
They hog the puck.

What happened when an icicle landed on the hockey player's head?
It knocked him out cold.

WORDPLAY

OXYMORONS

An oxymoron, as you probably know, is a figure of speech that combines words that, when placed together, appear to contradict each other. The best-known ones include jumbo shrimp *and* old news. *Can you add any others to this list?*

- accidentally on purpose
- alone together
- clearly misunderstood
- cold sweat
- conspicuous absence
- crash landing
- deafening silence
- definite maybe
- down escalator
- drag race
- dull roar
- easy problem
- even odds
- exact opposite
- freezer burn
- genuine imitation
- growing smaller
- guest host
- hopeless optimist
- impossible solution

- larger half
- lengthy brief
- living legend
- loosely sealed
- loud whisper
- mud bath
- original copy
- permanent temp
- plastic glasses
- pretty ugly
- random order
- sad smile
- seriously funny
- sharp curve
- silent scream
- small crowd
- weirdly normal
- working vacation

PALINDROMES

Palindrome: a word, a phrase, or a sentence sequence that reads the same backward and forward. Examples include madam *and* nurses run. *The number 1881 is also a palindrome. Classic examples are* Madam I'm Adam *(how Adam introduced himself to Eve);* A man, a plan, a canal—Panama; *and* Able was I ere I saw Elba *(supposedly said by Napoleon in captivity). Can you add any to this list?*

- civic
- deed
- deified
- kayak
- level
- no lemons, no melon
- pop
- racecar
- radar
- repaper
- rotator
- see referees
- step on no pets
- trapeze part
- was it a car or a cat I saw?

SILENT LETTER SCRAMBLES

Rearrange the letters of each word to get a new word that starts with a silent letter.

- grown
- hangs
- keen
- lamps
- naked
- swelter
- tower
- trinket

TOM SWIFTIES

This is a type of wordplay in which there is a punning connection between an adverb and the statement it refers to. Here are some examples. Try coming up with your own Tom Swifties. (Hint: Most adverbs end with –ly.)

"Camping is so much fun," said Tom intensely.

"Don't go near the turtle," Tom said snappingly.

"Get to the back of the ship," Tom commanded sternly.

"I can't find the melon," Tom said fruitlessly.

"I love hockey," Tom said puckishly.

"I really like hotdogs," said Tom with relish.

"I'll have the lamb chops," Tom said to the waiter sheepishly.

"I'm a terrible dart player," Tom said aimlessly.

"I'm the team's pitcher," Tom announced underhandedly.

"I'm your new supervisor," Tom said bossily.

"Pass me the shellfish," Tom said crabbily.

"Please pass the potato chips," Tom said crisply.

GROANER ALERT

Bonus points for rolled eyes

What has a bottom at the top?
Your legs.

What gets bigger the more you take away?
A hole.

I have a neck but no head. I have two arms but no hands. What am I?
A shirt.

What room has no floor, no walls, no doors, and no ceiling?
A mushroom.

Why do hummingbirds hum?
Because they don't know the words.

Waiter, waiter, this coffee tastes like dirt!
Well, it was just ground this morning.

I can cut down a tree just by looking at it.
I saw it with my own two eyes.

Nap on the forest floor.
You'll sleep like a log.

One bird can't make a pun, but toucan.

People kept telling me to stop imitating a flamingo. Finally, I just had to put my foot down.

I took a picture of a wheat field today. It came out pretty grainy.

I was wondering . . . Why can't hedgehogs just share the hedge?

I can recognize twenty-five letters of the alphabet. I just don't know why.

Nineteen got into a fight with twenty and twenty won.

Turning vegan is a big missed steak.

I'm reading a book about antigravity. It is impossible to put down!

Ontario's provincial bird got married because it was tired of being a loon.

BEHEADED

When you behead a word, you remove the first letter—and then you have another word. To play, give clues for both words, the longer word first. Example: "Originally, it smells sweet [flower]. Beheaded, it's to reduce in value [lower]."

It's fun to come up with interesting and challenging clues. Try to find pairs of words with very different meanings, words with connected meanings, and words that don't sound alike.

Here are a few more examples:

Originally it's to shut. Beheaded it's to misplace. (close, lose)

Originally it's a tragedy. Beheaded it's a comedy. (slaughter, laughter)

Originally, it's to stay away from. Beheaded it's emptiness. (avoid, void)

Originally it's fresh. Beheaded it's stale. (bold, old)

Originally it isn't here. Beheaded it isn't there. (there, here).

BALDERDASH

All you need are some paper and pens and a dictionary to play this favourite bluffing game. One player—the moderator—selects an unknown word from the dictionary, writes down its definition, and reads just the word out loud. Players each write down a made-up, but believable, definition and hand their papers to the moderator. The moderator then reads out the real answer and all the made-up ones, in random order. The other players must guess which definition is actually correct. The first person to guess correctly becomes the next person to moderate and read the mystery word.

OUTDOOR FUN

Set up a horseshoe pit, a bocce ball lane, or a croquet course.

Scavenger hunt: have the kids gather objects from nature such as pine cones, driftwood, snail shells, and coloured stones.

ABCs of nature: find a natural object for each letter of the alphabet (or as many letters as possible), starting with A—a fun game to play on a hike.

ART FROM NATURE

Cut a piece of fruit and you'll find a pattern. (An apple has a star design.) Or use vegetables with interesting textures, such as corn on the cob. Pour different colours of washable paint (tempera) onto paper plates and dip in the fruit or vegetable. Then press it onto paper—and voilà! A beautiful pattern! Glitter can add sparkle to the page. Fruits you can use include apples, pears, oranges, bananas, and lemons. For vegetables, try broccoli, cauliflower, carrots, corn on the cob, Brussels sprouts, and mushrooms.

Collect pretty or unusual plants or leaves and mount them on heavy paper or a board. With a simple frame or by placing the paper or board under glass, you'll create a piece of wall art or an attractive tabletop.

DOGGONE FUNNY

You've cat to be kitten me!

How do you keep a dog from barking in the back seat of a car?
Put her in the front seat.

Mandy: You play Scrabble with your dog? He must be supersmart.
Andy: Not really. I usually win.

What animals like bowling? Alley cats.

Why are dogs such terrible dancers?
Because they have two left feet.

What do cats call mice? Delicious.

What kind of dog enjoys taking baths?
The shampoodle.

What do you get when you cross a cat with a parrot?
A carrot.

Doctor, doctor. I feel like a dog.
Sit!

Did you hear about the cat that ate a ball of wool?
She had mittens.

Why did the cat family move next door to the mouse family?
So they could have the neighbours over for dinner.

Sonia: My dog doesn't have a nose.
Steve: How does she smell?
Sonia: Terrible.

What do cats like for breakfast?
Mice Krispies.

Why do dogs run in circles?
Because it's too hard to run in squares.

Lee: I've lost my dog.
Bea: Why don't you put an ad in the newspaper?
Lee: I don't think that would help—my dog can't read.

What do cats put in their milk to keep it cold?
Mice cubes.

Two fleas were on their way home from the movies. The first one said to the other, "Should we walk or take a dog?"

GHOST

The objective of this word game is to not spell out a word.
This game requires two or more players.

- The first player thinks of a word and then says the first letter out loud.

- The next player adds a letter—and must be thinking of a real word that has that first and that second letter.

- The third person adds a letter—and makes sure the three letters do not spell a word. The letters still need to be part of a longer real word. The game continues in this way. As the letters add up, it gets harder to avoid spelling out a word when a letter is added.

- The first person who is forced to spell out a word (or who spells one out accidentally) gets a *G* (the first letter in *GHOST*), and the next player starts a new round.

- If a person is stuck and cannot think of a letter to add, they can fake it and say any letter that doesn't complete a word. But the next person can challenge that player. And if the player can't come up with a word, then they get a *G*. If the player does come up with a word, then the challenger gets a *G*.

- The first person to lose five times and spell out *GHOST* loses. The game continues until there is just one winner.

LEGEN-DAIRY LAFFS

Old MacDonald had a funnybone....
E-I-E-I-HO-HO-HO

What did the mother cow say to the calf?
It's pasture bedtime.

What do cows do after school?
They go to the moo-vies.

What do you give a sick pig?
Oinkment.

What's got four legs and goes "Boo!"?
A cow with a cold.

What do you get when you cross a dinosaur with a pig?
Jurassic Pork.

What does a cow eat that's made with cheese curds and gravy?
Moo-tine.

Why did the hockey fans wait in a rainy field of wheat?
They wanted to see Grain Wetzky.

How do you learn about ice cream?
You go to sundae school.

Did you hear the joke about poutine?
It's really cheesy.

What's Winnie's favourite meal?
Pooh-tine.

Did you hear about the ghost who wanted french fries, cheese curds, and gravy?
He walked into a restaurant and asked for boo-tine.

What do you call a cow that can't make milk?
A milk dud.

Why did the cow cross the road?
To get to the udder side.

What do you call a cow who just won the lottery?
A cash cow.

Why did the cow look so confused?
She was having déjà-moo.

What do you call a sleeping cow?
A bull dozer.

COMMITTEE LIMERICKS

A limerick, we know, is a silly poem with five lines, and it's often funny or nonsensical. Limericks follow a certain rhyme and syllable pattern. The first, second, and fifth lines rhyme with each other and have the same number of syllables (usually eight or nine). The third and fourth lines rhyme with each other and also have the same number of syllables (usually five or six).

dah-DAH dah-dah-DAH dah-dah-DAH
dah-DAH dah-dah-DAH dah-dah-DAH
dah-DAH dah-dah-DAH
dah-DAH dah-dah-DAH
dah-DAH dah-dah-DAH dah-dah-DAH

With two to five players, you can write a "committee limerick," with one person coming up with the first line, the next person coming up with the second line, and so on. Here are a few first lines to get you started:

There was a young fellow named Stu . . .
A woman from Sault Ste. Marie . . .
My history teacher was sad . . .

TONGUE TWISTERS

Say each phrase quickly, at least three times. Try to trip up your friends too!

A proper copper coffee pot

Blake the baker bakes black bread

Five frantic frogs fled from fifty fierce fishes

Hippos hiccup

How can a clam cram in a clean cream can?

Irish wristwatch, Swiss wristwatch

Moose noshing much mush

Peggy Babcock

Red leather, yellow leather

Sheena leads, Sheila needs

The quack quit asking quick questions

Toy boat, toy boat

Willy's real rear wheel

Ed had edited it

Twelve twins twirled twelve twigs

GROANER ALERT

What are you groaning on about?

Why did the sheep change direction?
It wanted to make a ewe turn.

How do farmers make crop circles?
They use a pro-tractor.

How many chocolate bars can you eat on an empty stomach?
Only one. After that, your stomach won't be empty.

What happened to the dinosaur after he took the school bus home?
He had to bring it back.

Which side of a tiger has the most stripes?
The outside.

What is easy to get into but hard to get out of?
Trouble.

What question can you never answer yes to?
Are you asleep yet?

I never suspected my dad stole items he found on highway posts, but when I got home, all the signs were there.

Don't steal kitchen utensils, unless it's a whisk you're willing to take.

I didn't think that pigs could fly until the swine flu.

The inventor of the door knocker won a no-bell prize.

German sausage jokes are just the wurst.

I spotted a lion at the zoo, so now he looks like a leopard.

If money doesn't grow on trees, why do banks have branches?

My left side went missing—but I'm all right now.

The Bay of Fundy is really strong becasue it's full of mussels.

PUN FUN

See if you can come up with some more of these:

A boiled egg is hard to beat.

A thief who stole a calendar got twelve months.

He had a photographic memory that was never developed.

The batteries were given out free of charge.

The guy who fell onto an upholstery machine is now fully recovered.

When a clock is hungry, it goes back four seconds.

When fish are in schools, they sometimes take debate.

When you've seen one shopping centre, you've seen a mall.

THE LICENCE PLATE GAME

On the road to the cottage, watch for the letters on the licence plates you see. The objective of the game is to spell a word using the letters in the order they appear— no rearranging. You can play by yourself or with as many people as fit in the car with you! The person who creates the longest word wins. Here are some examples to get you started:

FOUR-LETTER PLATES

ARCD	abracadabra
GVAN	galvanize
CBLE	combustible

THREE-LETTER PLATES

VPE	envelope
BTE	unbeatable
JNI	juniper

LAKEHOUSE LAUGHS

Where does cottage cheese go to relax?
Far, far a-whey.

What kind of materials do dinosaurs use for the floors of their cottages?
Rep-tiles.

Why did the teacher jump into the lake?
Because he wanted to test the water.

What did the fishin' magician say?
Pick a cod, any cod.

Do fish ever go on vacation?
No—they are always in school.

How do you catch a school of fish?
With bookworms.

What did the beaver say to the maple tree?
It's been nice gnawing you.

What do you call a polar bear in New Brunswick?
Lost.

What animal is always at a baseball game?
A bat.

How does the moon cut his hair?
Eclipse it.

What can you hold without using your hands?
Your breath.

What fish tastes best with peanut butter?
Jellyfish.

Why are frogs so good at basketball?
Because they always make jump shots.

What do you get when you cross a bear with a skunk?
Winnie the Pee-yew!

What's a rabbit's favourite airline?
Hare Canada.

What do fireflies say at the start of a race?
Ready. Set. Glow!

What sound do porcupines make when they kiss?
Ouch!

I LIKE COFFEE, BUT I DON'T LIKE TEA

This game is fun for a small group. You could start by saying, "I like coffee, but I don't like tea. I like puddles, but I don't like rain. I like boots, but I don't like shoes." The other players try to figure out why you like one thing but not another. In this example, you like things with double letters (double *f* in *coffee*, double *d* in *puddles*, double *o* in *boots*). You keep giving examples until a player guesses why you like one thing but not the other. Another example is one-syllable words versus two ("I like apples, but I don't like pears. I like pencils, but I don't like pens."). Or you can use words with the letter *q* ("I like quizzes, but I don't like puzzles. I like squares, but I don't like circles."). Or words without the letter *a*, words spelled with four letters, or any other patterns you can think of.

"HOW DID WE FIT THIS ALL IN
ON THE WAY HERE?"

—Perplexed and Packing

Campfire Stories

ACE IN THE HOLE

Why the most ornate card in the pack is still the ace of spades.

We associate counterfeiters with banknotes, but there have been many other profitable ways to counterfeit valuable papers. One of the more unusual crimes was forging playing cards.

Beginning in the 1500s, playing cards in England were subject to a large tax. To prove the tax had been paid, a stamp would be placed on the outside of the pack. A second mark was also placed on the ace of spades—a card that was printed only on government presses, and whose design had the sort of intricacy you'd see on a banknote.

By 1710, 95 percent of the price of a pack of cards was tax. Predictably, the people who made and sold these decks of cards wondered if there was a way to game the system and keep more of the price for themselves.

Richard Harding was a playing card manufacturer in the early 1800s. Harding ran two shops selling cards in London,

and like all his colleagues, he purchased "duty cards"—the licensed aces—from the government printers. His shops did a brisk trade, but government agents noticed he wasn't buying as many aces as they expected. They investigated his business and examined his cards more closely. His aces were forged. After searching the properties of his associates, they discovered the printing plates he'd used to make the fake cards.

In 1805, Harding was tried for counterfeiting and selling the cards, found guilty, and sentenced to death. The government took this crime very seriously. Despite calls for him to be spared, he was hanged at Newgate prison. The case had been in all the papers, and a huge crowd turned out for the execution.

Despite the fearsome penalties, Harding wasn't the only one trying to get around the card duty. Around the same time, a twenty-eight-year-old printer named John Blacklin figured he had

found a safer way to avoid the tax. He sold bargain-priced decks of fifty-one playing cards—all the cards except the expensive ace of spades. And if you happened to be one of those picky players who wanted to complete the set, he also sold packets with a dozen not-entirely-official aces of spades. With one ace-of-spades set and a stack of incomplete decks, you could buy a lot of cards without paying any tax.

The way Blacklin saw it, the scheme was pure genius.

Or maybe not.

When agents got wind of the scheme, Blacklin was arrested and hauled before a judge. His lawyers argued that the aces weren't taxable on their own, and neither were the incomplete decks. The court was not convinced; as far as they were concerned, the aces were forged. Blacklin was convicted of "feloniously vending playing cards." He was also sentenced to death.

The tax on cards continued in the UK until 1960, although by then nobody was being hanged for violations. The amount of the tax hadn't kept up with inflation, and when someone calculated that the cost of collecting the tax was more than the money the government was making from it, the card tax was dropped for good.

Despite the disappearance of the tax, the laws influence the design of playing cards even today. In many packs, the most ornate card is still the ace of spades.

THE CAR
ON THE RIVER

She snapped some selfies as her car
sank lower into the water.

Manotick is a small town in the countryside, not far from Ottawa. It lies on the Rideau River. The people who live along the waterfront can take their kayaks and canoes out in the summer. In winter, it can be a great place to skate or play hockey.

On a cold January day in 2022, a group of kids were playing hockey on an outdoor rink on the river's edge. Suddenly, they were startled by the sound of a car's engine behind them. They turned in astonishment to see a small yellow car, a Scion tC, speeding over the ice at close to 120 kilometres an hour, using the frozen waterway as a private expressway.

According to CTV News, the driver was a young woman. It's not known whether she was thrill-seeking or thought the frozen river was a suitable road. She may have been driving for quite a distance—one observer said they'd seen her zipping by earlier, some thirty kilometers away. Whatever she thought, she was making a dangerous mistake. Moments after she passed the kids, the car skidded. The vehicle went through the ice and quickly started to fill with frigid water.

One resident, Zachary, talked to a local radio host about the event. He said he had been out on the ice with his wife, teaching their toddler to skate, when they saw the car speed by and crash.

Zachary bundled up the child, while his wife ran towards the crash site. It didn't look good. She saw that the car had plunged through the ice into the middle of the fast-running river. The ice around the car had broken away. The woman urged the driver to climb out of the vehicle and get on the roof. The driver's-side window was open, but the driver was preoccupied with putting her possessions into a duffel bag. After some frantic calls—"Forget your stuff! Get out of the car!"—the young driver squeezed through the window and stood on top of the car. Incredibly, she was still dry, and she seemed amused by her predicament. She snapped some selfies as her car sank lower into the water.

Zachary and his neighbours arrived on the scene. One had already phoned for emergency services, but the car was sinking so fast they were afraid they'd run out of time.

The driver seemed blissfully unaware of how dangerous an icy river can be, both for those who fall through the ice and for would-be rescuers. But the neighbours knew the dangers all too well. If the driver went into the water in this fast current, she could easily be pulled under the ice. Even if she didn't drown, just a few minutes of hypothermia can lead to death. The car was surrounded by water, with loose chunks of ice all around it. There was no way the driver could jump from the car to an area of solid ice.

Zachary had brought a piece of plywood to use in a rescue, but it was clear they needed something better.

One of the neighbours spotted a metal canoe on a lawn, but it was frozen to the ground, and they couldn't budge it. Zachary's neighbour Bill said he had a kayak back at his place—perhaps they could use that to pull the driver back to shore. It was a smart plan. A kayak should slide well over ice, and if the ice broke, it would still float on the water. But time was running out. While Bill ran to take the kayak from its rack, Zachary uncoiled a length of yellow rope.

The car was still steadily sinking, and its driver was still heedlessly snapping selfies. Only the roof of the car was above the water now.

Bill and Zachary tied the rope to the little blue kayak, and then, as a group of worried bystanders looked on, they slid it out across the ice, then across the water surrounding the car. The men called to the driver to get on the kayak. She took a break from her photo shoot to step down onto it. The rescue came not a moment too soon. The car disappeared under the water.

Zachary and Bill hauled on the rope, pulling the driver smoothly over the water, across the ice, and back to the safety of the shore.

Emergency crews arrived on the scene moments later—they were fast, but in this case, they might not have been fast enough to save the driver's life. Police were impressed by the efficient rescue carried out by the neighbours. The Ottawa Police dive team later tweeted: "Thankfully no injuries and an amazing job by local residents saving the driver by using a kayak and quick safe thinking."

The car was later extracted from the river. It took chainsaws to cut through the ice, and then a heavy-duty tow truck to pull the car out. As for its snap-happy driver, the *Manotick Messenger* later reported that she was charged with dangerous operation of a motor vehicle.

It's a long-standing practice for players of street hockey to shout "Car!" as a vehicle comes down the road, but as one of the residents said, "You don't expect your kids to have to watch out for cars zipping down on the frozen river."

GHOSTS
OF THE YUKON

He had been about to make what could have been a deadly mistake with explosives when the ghost miner appeared and gave a warning.

Canada's wilderness has its share of ghost stories, and as you head out further into the sparsely populated regions of the north, the stories become more peculiar.

An article in the *Yukoner Magazine* tells of a ghostly encounter in 1964. Dave, a seventeen-year-old, had been hired at a silver mine in the town of Elsa. He was working with another man, an Italian named Nick. The boss called them over and gave them a job—there was an old shaft, 150 metres below ground, that had been shut down. The boss wanted them to go to that shaft and remove any equipment that could be reused.

They did as they were asked and went to the old shaft, but when they arrived, they immediately discovered a problem. An old mining ore cart was off the rails, blocking the entrance.

Nick said the cart was much too heavy to lift—they would need some sturdy poles and wedges to lever it back onto the rails. He went off to find the equipment in another part of the mine, leaving Dave waiting by the cart.

While Nick was gone, another miner appeared and seemed interested in what Dave was up to. Dave explained the problem. The miner got behind the cart and started lifting. Dave joined him, and together they managed to shift the heavy cart and get it back on the rails. Once the work was done, the miner walked back up the shaft.

Moments later, Nick returned bearing the poles. He was amazed to find the cart back on the rails and Dave standing nearby grinning. Nick asked Dave how on earth he had managed to move the heavy cart on his own. Dave admitted he had had help from the other miner.

Nick asked who he meant. Dave said the guy who just left—Nick must have passed him on the way.

Nick went pale. He told Dave there was no other miner in the shaft. But, he continued, there were stories of a ghost miner, a man who had died in this very shaft a few years ago. The way Nick saw it, Dave had just had help from a dead man.

Dave laughed at Nick's superstitious beliefs. But later, he talked to other miners on the site, trying to find the man who had helped him. It was just like Nick had said, nobody else had been in that shaft, although several miners had their own stories of a strange figure who stepped in to help them, then mysteriously disappeared. One miner told Dave he had been about to make what could have been a deadly mistake with explosives when the ghost miner appeared and gave a warning. Except it wasn't exactly a warning—when he thought back on the conversation afterwards, he realized no words had been spoken.

When Dave thought about it, he couldn't remember his visitor speaking out loud either. He just understood the other man's intentions. And his actions spoke for themselves.

* * *

Not all ghosts in the Yukon have the power to move objects. Some just bring bad news.

In the book *I Married the Klondike*, Laura Beatrice Berton (mother of historian and TV presenter Pierre Berton) described her life in Dawson City, Yukon, and recounted a strange story about the town's best-known physician, Dr. Lachapelle. The doctor, an energetic character who had lived there since the days of the gold rush, was well liked by

the community. He had treated many of the townsfolk, and attended his share of deaths too. Many of the town's death certificates from the early 1900s bear Lachapelle's signature.

Dr. Lachapelle was an experienced outdoorsman and a keen hunter, and in September 1924, he travelled upriver to shoot some game at Stewart Crossing, nearly 160 kilometres from Dawson. He took his dog for company—a cocker spaniel named Rufus.

He spent a couple of weeks away hunting and bagged plenty of ducks and geese. When he was done, Lachapelle said goodbye to the man who ran the roadhouse near Stewart Crossing, then climbed into his canoe and let the river carry him home.

Dr. Lachapelle had a housekeeper, a Japanese woman who remained at his big house in Dawson City, looking after the place while the doctor was away on his canoe trip. One day, while she was working, she heard the sound of a door opening by the kitchen. She went to see who had entered the house. She was shocked to see Dr. Lachapelle standing there, pale and dripping with water. As she moved towards him to ask what was going on, the doctor vanished.

The housekeeper ran out of the house screaming. She told a neighbour what she had seen. The neighbour dismissed the story, and rumours spread around town that the housekeeper had gone a little crazy.

But later, people in Dawson started to think twice about her experience. Dr. Lachapelle was late in returning. Then a piece of alarming news reached the townsfolk—a police patrol had found a wrecked canoe on a sandbar along the Yukon River.

A few weeks later, the doctor's dog turned up at the Stewart Crossing roadhouse. The poor animal was in a terrible state—bedraggled and half-starved.

The little dog was returned to its Dawson home. When locals saw the doctor's pet without its loving master, they were convinced the doctor must have died in the wilderness. No remains were ever found. Dr. Lachapelle probably drowned in the ice-cold waters of the Yukon—although they said it was impossible to be sure without a body.

His housekeeper, however, had no doubt that he had drowned. She had seen his dead body when it visited the house.

THE LOST NOMADS

I feel like I know these guys.

It was a Friday the 13th, December 1940, when the Royal Canadian Air Force personnel at Camp Borden got news that one of their trainee pilots had gone missing. It would be the first of a string of very unfortunate events.

Camp Borden, near Barrie, Ontario, is today known as CFB Borden. During the Second World War, areas that are now considered cottage country were a training site for pilots. Allied officers from across Canada, Britain, and other parts of the world went there to learn the skills they would need to fly over Europe. The region's forests and lakes were a good match for the conditions pilots might face over Scandinavia or Germany.

Leading Aircraftman Clayton Peder Hopton had come to Camp Borden from Saskatchewan. He'd nearly finished his training, and he was just a day away from receiving his pilot wings, along with the rest of his classmates. On December 13, he was out on one last formation flight. His flight commander spotted bad weather ahead and gave instructions for all planes to bank right so they could avoid the storm. Hopton must have missed the instruction. Instead of turning with the formation, he flew right into the clouds. He hadn't been seen since.

By evening, there was still no trace of Hopton. The Royal Canadian Air Force organized a huge search, spending the night assigning search sectors to the west and north of Camp Borden. The next morning, at daybreak, a mass of planes took to the air. Hopton's classmates were among the volunteers—many had given up their leave in order to participate in the search.

Hopton, however, was already dead. He had likely become disoriented in the thick clouds. It can happen all too easily: surrounded by clouds, a pilot may think he's flying level but be descending rapidly. A farmer later reported that he saw Hopton's plane dive down behind some trees. The pilot must have died instantly. He left behind a young bride—they had married in secret just two months earlier.

Those searching for Hopton knew none of this. They also didn't know that more tragedy was to follow.

Two planes in the search had flown out to check a sector in the Muskoka region. Each pilot flew a Northrop Λ17Λ Nomad. It was an unusual aircraft—a single-engine plane, designed for use as a light bomber. The planes had originally been built for the French military, but before they could be delivered, France fell to the Germans. The RCAF purchased the planes instead. The British and Canadian Air Force were moving towards bombers with multiple engines by then, so the Nomad's design was starting to look outdated, but the planes were useful as advanced trainers.

The two planes searching around Muskoka were flown by experienced pilots, Flight Sergeant Lionel Francis and Flight Lieutenant Peter Campbell. In the back of each two-seater aircraft was a trainee pilot—Leading Aircraftmen William Gosling and Theodore Scribner Bates.

The flyers completed searching the sector assigned to them but found no trace of Hopton's plane. They were ordered to take their Nomads in for a landing at Muskoka Airfield.

Flying conditions were good that day, but as the two planes flew in forma-tion over Lake Muskoka, preparing for their landing, something went wrong. One plane collided with the other. Both planes fell from the sky and plunged into the lake.

All four men died in the crash. Divers later recovered one aircraft, and the bodies of Leading Aircraftman Gosling and Flight Sergeant Francis were recovered and interred, but the other plane was lost. The second plane, Nomad 3521, was presumed to be at the bottom of the lake, but there was no way to find it.

The bodies of Flight Lieutenant Campbell and Leading Aircraftman Bates could not be returned to their grieving families.

People assumed the plane and its crew would remain forever at the bottom of the lake. But they didn't count on the tenacity of a Muskoka local named Matt Fairbrass.

In 2001, Matt Fairbrass read about the tragic accident and the missing plane. Technology had advanced over the decades, and Matt wondered whether it might be possible to find the lost Nomad using modern methods. After all, fishermen could use sonar gear to detect fish. Perhaps similar equipment could be used to find the plane. He teamed up with his friend Al Bacon, and some skilled associates from "the Lost Airmen in Muskoka Project," and they began a systematic sonar scan of the lake.

CAMPFIRE STORIES

After their activities were written up in the local paper, Fairbrass received a letter from a man in Guelph who said his brother had been one of those on the lost plane. The more he learned, the more personal the search became. The searchers spent hundreds of hours scanning the lakebed, in a back-and-forth sweep that partner Al Bacon described as "like mowing a lawn."

They eventually identified three signals that seemed like they might correspond to the lost plane, but taking things further would require more resources than they could afford. They went to the OPP and presented their data. The police were surprised and impressed by the quality of the information Fairbrass and his associates had put together. The police officers shared Matt's passion for finding the lost aircraft—after all, the plane's occupants were still "missing persons."

After more scanning and more searching, divers from the OPP's Underwater Search and Recovery Unit discovered the wreckage in 2010. The Department of Defence got involved then, and in 2012, the remains of the lost airmen were finally recovered. They were laid to rest, in adjacent plots, at Guelph's Woodlawn Memorial Park Cemetery.

Those attending the ceremony included Tom Bates, the younger brother of Leading Aircraftman Bates. Also attending was Matt Fairbrass. He described the experience as "surreal." After spending so many years hunting for the missing airmen, learning about their stories and their families, he was now looking at their coffins, their bodies recovered from the lake's depths thanks, in part, to his work. He said, "I feel like I know these guys."

Two years later, the lost plane was recovered from the silt at the bottom of the lake. It has not yet been determined what will be done with the plane, but it has been proposed that the wreckage could be shown to the public with its pieces arranged as they were on the lakebed, as another reminder of the crew who lost their lives there.

IT'S THE SUN, SON

The sunlight entering your eyes now may have left the sun about eight minutes back, but it was created inside the sun about a quarter of a million years ago.

The next time you're out fishing on a lake on a hot, sunny day, take a moment to think about the sun.

The sun is a gigantic mass of hydrogen and helium, plus a smattering of other chemicals, all pulled into a ball by its own gravity. The atoms in its centre are pressed hard by the weight of all the stuff above them. That pressure is so strong that some atoms get crushed together, two combining into one in a flash of light and heat, and that's why the sun shines. Physicists have been trying to do the same trick on earth for years—some cynics say that fusion is fifty years away, and always will be. In the meantime, the fusion reactor in the sky blazes away without the need for engineers and gives us that whole "life on earth" experience.

The sun is in a perpetual state of turmoil. Across its roiling surface, hot, glowing gases rise up from deep below, cool, then go tumbling down again, forming currents and patterns that resemble the turbulent surface of miso soup. Sometimes darker spots form on the surface where magnetic forces briefly make a region slightly cooler. Sometimes, flares flash out, stretching and looping thousands of kilometres above the surface like a cosmic bullwhip.

But despite the explosive violence of all these reactions, our sun is a remarkably stable star. It keeps shining reliably, steadily, hardly varying in the amount of heat it puts out. The sun's core is something like 15 million degrees Celsius, but its temperature is rock solid, varying by only a dozen degrees up or down, and it has stayed steady for millions of years.

Not every star works that way. Some stars get hotter and cooler at regular intervals. If our planet were in orbit around a star like that, oceans would freeze, then boil, and we wouldn't be here at all.

Our sun was born 4.6 billion years ago, emerging out of a huge cloud of

material, a "stellar nursery," that produced many similar stars. The galaxy has swirled around twenty times since then, and the sun's siblings have become separated. It would be amazing to find them—after all, if our sun supports life, maybe those stars do as well. It might even be that early life from Earth was blown out into space and landed on planets around those sister stars. A few years back, astronomers found one star they believe is one of the sun's lost siblings. Now they're trying to see if it has planets.

For all its dependability, the sun still has many mysteries and surprises. For example, scientists can't understand why some parts are as hot as they are.

The very hottest part of the sun, as you might expect, is the nuclear furnace in its centre. It cools as you go further out, and the surface of the sun, hot though it is, is much cooler than the centre. The surface of the sun is more than 5,000 degrees Celsius, which is pretty cool, as far as the sun is concerned. But, strangely, as you leave the sun and go further out, the sun's atmosphere gets hotter again, and then it gets very hot—more than a million degrees. Why is that? What's going on to make the sun's atmosphere so much hotter than the shining surface below? Nobody knows.

When we look at the sun and moon in the sky, they appear about the same size—that's why a solar eclipse works as well as does. But the sun is so much further away than the moon that it's hard to get your head around the distances. Put it this way: if you could get in your car and drive to the moon at highway speeds, the trip would take you about twenty-two weeks. The same trip to the sun would take close to 170 years—so make sure you bring snacks. And sunscreen.

Even light takes a while to get from the sun's surface to you. When you see the sun in the sky, you're seeing our star the way it looked eight minutes ago, because that's roughly how long it takes for light to travel from the surface of the sun to your sunbathing body or dazzled eyes. If the sun suddenly went out right now, it would take us eight minutes to be aware of it.

But what's really surprising is how long it takes that light to make the much shorter trip from the sun's core to its surface. It is unbelievably slow. Each little photon bounces its way from atom to atom, crawling its way through the sun's dense interior. The sunlight entering your eyes now may have left the sun about eight minutes back, but it was created inside the sun about a quarter of a million years ago.

We think of the sun as having a yellowish colour, but that's a trick of the atmosphere. If you were to go up into space, you would see that the sun is perfectly white and gives off what photographers and artists would call a "cold" light. You can see it when you look at those old Apollo photographs from the moon. The stark lighting makes the moon appear like a frozen wasteland, although those thick astronaut suits are protecting the astronauts from a blaze of sunlight that would boil their blood in seconds.

A lot of the sunlight we see is second-hand. When sunlight hits the air above us, it makes the sky glow like a neon tube, as the blue and violet in its light strikes the oxygen and nitrogen in our atmosphere and get scattered out again as a glowing expanse of sky.

Before dawn, we see the first traces of sunlight, after it's gone through the air over the horizon. All the blue has been filtered out and we see only reds and oranges at first, with a deep blue in the higher areas where the air is thinner. The glow spreads and shifts in colour as the sun's light strikes our patch of the sky more directly, and colours shift until we finally see the glow of a familiar blue sky, shining so brightly that it is no longer possible to see the glow of the stars above.

At night, the process is reversed. Blues become darker, and the glow changes back through yellow, orange, and red.

Still, nothing lasts forever, even the sun's steady temperature. If you would prefer a warmer sun, you can have it if you stick around long enough. Our sun is very slowly heating up. We've got about a billion years until it gets so hot that all the water on earth will boil away.

Enjoy your fishing while you can.

SHIPWRECKED
IN NEWFOUNDLAND

*It was survival of the fittest, but in this case
it proved to be the un-fittest who survived.*

Today, we look on the wilderness as something to be treasured, enjoyed, and protected, but for Europeans in the 1800s, the vast emptiness of Canada's wilderness was often a source of terror.

In 1805, a troopship with the (unfortunate) name of HMS *Aeneas* was on its way to North America. Aside from the crew, the ship carried over three hundred passengers—soldiers moving to Canada with their families. They were bound for Quebec, where the new arrivals would reinforce the garrison already there.

The ship was part of a large convoy, including transports, merchant ships, and warships. The vessels travelled together for protection against the French privateers that were raiding British ships.

The Atlantic crossing should have taken a month—the convoy left England at the end of August, and the soldiers expected to arrive in Quebec by the end of September. But bad weather followed

them all the way. The convoy struggled against storms and heavy seas. As September came to a close, they were still in the middle of the Atlantic. And they were still at sea as the end of October approached, still crawling towards Newfoundland.

Weather conditions were so bad that the convoy had difficulty staying together. Worse, the trip had taken so long that ships were running out of water and food. Passengers were weakened by the constant tossing of the ocean, and infectious disease started spreading among the crowded troopships.

One ship, named *Two Friends*, carried forty soldiers and all the regiment's heavy equipment. It ran into heavy fog and was blown onto a reef off Cape Breton. Those aboard could see land but they were unable to reach it, and water was flooding into the hold. The crew fought to keep the ship from blowing back out to sea, where it would certainly have sunk, drowning everyone aboard. Cape Breton locals spotted the wreck and sent out a small boat to save those aboard. Three drowned, but the locals managed to shuttle all the rest to land before the ship was finally swept back out to sea. The ship was lost, along with all the regiment's gear. But it turned out that those on the *Two Friends* were the lucky ones. The next day, another vessel would be lost.

The HMS *Aeneas* had fallen far behind the other ships. As it rolled and lurched around the south coast of Newfoundland, the ship struck a rock with tremendous force. It was four in the morning. The skies were black and a tremendous wind was blowing. The passengers were panicked by the sudden jolt, knowing immediately the ship was in trouble. Hundreds ran up onto the deck. While they were gathered there, several huge waves struck the ship, crashing high over the decks and washing countless people into the water.

The ship had run aground near Isle aux Morts. The name means Island of the Dead, for all the shipwrecks and deaths that had occurred in the region. It certainly lived up to its name that night. Only thirty-five people reached land. The rest were swept out to sea and never seen again.

Even the survivors were only at the start of their ordeal. They soon realized they had not reached the mainland but were stranded on a small, rocky islet. There was no shelter from the elements

there, and they huddled on the rocks in the dark. Some died overnight from injuries or exposure.

The next day, the rest of the survivors put their frozen hands to work building a raft from the ship's wreckage. They were successful and used the craft to cross to the mainland.

But once they were finally ashore and looked at the land they had reached, their hearts sank. The shipwrecked crew found themselves in the cold, storm-lashed wilderness of coastal Newfoundland. There was no sign of human habitation, just rock and forest, as far as the eye could see. Far from towns or settlements, they had no shelter and no food. They were cold, sick, and exhausted.

Despite their dire situation, many survivors displayed extraordinary bravery. One man, who had suffered two broken legs, crawled away to hide from the rest of the group so he wouldn't be a burden to them and harm their chances of survival. Another, a ship's boy, had exhausted himself trying to support an injured army major across the water. The ship's boy and the major both died.

A young ensign named Faulkner took command. It was clear that, if they stayed put, they would all die. They must find civilization. Those who couldn't walk would need to be left behind. He set off with a group of around twenty, leaving the injured to fend for themselves.

As they marched, another officer, a Lieutenant Dawson, found himself unable to keep up with the group. He too was left behind, although because Dawson was an officer and a gentleman, two soldiers were assigned to remain with him and look after him, while the rest of the party went on. It was survival of the fittest.

In this case it proved to be the un-fittest who survived. A Newfoundland hunter named Michael Gillam happened to turn up at the area where the survivors had landed. He was amazed to find these sick and injured people, and he took them all back to his cabin, giving them food and medical attention. When they told Gillam there had been others in the group, Gillam went searching for them too. One of the people he found and rescued was the man with the broken legs who had crawled away to die. That man lost his feet to frostbite but survived.

The party that had gone exploring did not do so well. Lieutenant Dawson died in the wilderness, and the two soldiers who had remained with him then wandered through the forests, enduring storms and snow, until they were discovered by a party of hunters and rescued. The soldiers told the hunters about Ensign Faulkner's group. The hunters asked for details—which way had they gone? But the soldiers, who had been lost themselves, had no idea where to direct the hunters.

Ensign Faulkner's party was never seen again. It is thought they died of starvation or exposure in the wilderness.

When spring came, Gillam led his five survivors to Fortune Bay, where they got on a ship for Quebec. Of the 347 people who had set sail on that troopship, these five, and the two soldiers who had stayed with the lieutenant, were the only ones to reach their destination.

METEORS

*People are often puzzled about why a meteorologist
studies the weather and not meteors.*

Make a wish! There goes a
falling star.

Fortunately, it's not an
actual falling star—because that would be
the end of life on earth. No, it's a meteor,
and they are falling to earth all the time.
Most meteors are tiny and burn up in the
atmosphere, although they fall in such
quantities that their weight really adds up.
Every year, meteors add 15,000 tonnes of
material to the planet.

If you see a meteor flash by, keep
your eyes on that area of the sky for a
few seconds. Sometimes a single rock has
split into parts, and the first meteor may
be followed by one or two more on the
same path.

People are often puzzled about why
a meteorologist studies the weather and
not meteors. (The technical term for a
person who studies meteors is *meteoriti-
cist*, but if you use the word, you'll need
to explain it every time.) The reason for
the confusion is that *meteor* once meant
any event that happened in the heavens.
Wind was an aerial meteor. Rain, snow,
and hail were aqueous meteors. Auroras
and rainbows were luminous meteors.
And shooting stars, which looked like
they were made of fire, were called igne-
ous meteors. Those are the only ones we
still call meteors today.

The root of the word *meteor* means
"high," and meteors are extremely high.
Although witnesses in news reports
may claim a bright meteor passed "right
between those trees there," or "down the
street, just over the power lines," it's hard
to assess distances at night, and they are
almost certainly wrong. The glowing trail
of most meteors is 70 to 100 kilometres
above the ground, at the boundary between our atmosphere and space.

People didn't always understand that
this "atmospheric fire" was caused by a
solid object, or that its remnants could
fall to earth. The brilliant French scientist
Antoine Lavoisier examined a meteorite

in the 1760s. He was not impressed. In his expert opinion, it was just a rock that had been blackened and melted by lightning. In those days, the idea that rocks might fall from the heavens seemed as ridiculous and unscientific as a rain of cats. He is reputed to have dismissed the idea of meteors by saying, "Stones cannot fall from the sky, because there are no stones in the sky!"

Today, we know Lavoisier was wrong. There are indeed stones in the sky, and as they fall, they become meteors. Before a meteor starts its pyrotechnic display, it's called a *meteoroid*. That's just a smallish space rock, hurtling through space at tens of kilometers a second—much faster than any bullet. When the rock meets the earth's atmosphere, the air rushing against its surface immediately burns off the outer layers, producing the spectacular streaks we see in the night sky. Most meteors—especially the ones in meteor showers, are minuscule, like grains of sand, and they burn up completely in the atmosphere. Larger ones stick around long enough to reach the ground. Once it lands, the rock that remains is no longer called a meteor—it is promoted to the rank of *meteorite*.

In science fiction movies, a freshly landed meteorite looks like a glowing, red-hot rock surrounded by burning shrubs—an object that will instantly sear the hands of anyone foolish enough to touch it. But experts say this image is all wrong—freshly fallen meteorites are not usually hot at all. The rock has spent thousands or millions of years drifting through space, where it is extremely cold. While the rock is falling to earth, its exterior gets heated up so much that it vaporizes and burns, often leaving a long tail, but because all that glowing gas is swept away, it doesn't heat up the interior of the rock. In the same way that fiery heat shield of a returning space capsule protects the astronauts inside the ship, it's only the outside of the meteor that burns. The inside stays cool.

A second reason meteorites aren't usually hot is that the meteor doesn't keep burning all the way down. As it falls and burns, the friction of our atmosphere slows it down dramatically. Eventually, the burning stops and the tail disappears, but the rock is still fifteen or twenty kilometres above ground. It then falls a long way through the bitterly cold air high in the atmosphere.

Researchers don't usually find a meteorite immediately after it has landed, but every so often they get lucky. In 1927, a four-kilogram chunk landed in Tilden, Illinois. Those who touched it after it had landed remarked on how cold it felt. Others have reported finding fresh meteorites covered in frost.

If you see a meteor falling and want to retrieve it—don't bother. The meteor you see will land far away from you, and meteorites are extremely difficult to find. Only a few dozen are found each year—mostly in deserts, where their presence is obvious.

Randy Korotev is an American scientist and meteor expert. People regularly send him photos of rocks they think are meteors. They almost never are. He notes that rocks that mysteriously fall on people's property are usually about the right size for someone to have thrown.

Even if you never find a meteorite, you can still learn some things about a meteor by watching it carefully. When scientists in a laboratory want to know what an unknown substance is made of, one method is to place it in a hot flame. Different chemicals have distinctive ways of glowing and may shine with a certain colour.

A meteor does all that for you. It's burning as it flies through the air, and about 10 percent of meteors have a definite colour. These colours can give useful clues about the meteor's composition. Impress your friends by identifying the chemicals as it falls.

If the meteor burns with a yellow light, that is usually a sign it is rich in iron. An orange meteor likely contains some sodium. A purple or violet meteor means calcium, while nickel will produce a green glow, and a blue-white meteor contains magnesium.

The speed of a meteor also affects its colour. If you're lucky, you may see a vivid red meteor. These often move quite slowly. In this case, the glow comes not from chemicals in the meteor itself, but from oxygen and nitrogen in our atmosphere, heated up and changed to plasma as the meteor passes through.

If all this is too hard to remember, just say thoughtfully, "Ah yes, I believe that meteor is mostly rocky, with traces of iron and nickel." Most meteorites fit this description, so there's a good chance you'll be right, and if you're not, odds are that nobody will ever find the meteorite and correct you.

A LAST TRIP
TO THE COTTAGE

She had an ominous feeling that she knew what it meant.

Judy married into the Reynolds family in the 1950s. She was only twenty years old and seemed young for her age. She had never lived away from home. Her new husband, Bill, was fifteen years her senior. He had a house and a steady job working for the city. He impressed Judy, but he knew so much more about the world than she did, and she sometimes found herself intimidated by his greater knowledge and experience.

What made things worse for Judy's confidence was that Bill was the baby in a large and close-knit family. Her new brothers- and sisters-in-law were decades older than the young bride. Two had young grandchildren.

Judy was shy by nature, and at family gatherings, she hardly knew what to say. Everyone around her seemed so assured and confident, while she felt like she was just playing the role of the happy home-maker. She didn't feel like she knew what she was doing.

Her husband's family loved Judy though. They could see she was nervous, but she was very sweet. One of the older brothers teased her, but the others tried to welcome her into the family. Nobody tried harder than the oldest sister, Marion, who was one of those maternal types, a natural caregiver. She took Judy under her wing, giving her the encouragement and support she needed. Marion helped her sister-in-law with the tasks a wife was supposed to be good at in those days: how to oil a sewing machine, how to get the laundry done faster, and the secrets to some of the favourite family recipes—according to Marion, getting that right was the key to a successful marriage.

The hub of family activity was the cottage. It was actually three buildings—a house and two smaller cabins. It sat on a big plot of land running down to a small lake.

Bill and his brothers constantly worked on "improvements" there, fixing a boat shed or extending a deck. Half the work never seemed to get finished, but it was cheerful activity.

Judy had grown up in farm country, so she was comfortable with outdoor work, but this cottage life was new to her. Again, Marion stepped in to help. They went out in the canoe together. Judy started to appreciate the lifestyle. Before long, the trip to the cottage was one of her favourite activities.

The years went by, and when Judy had children, she brought them up to the cottage too, driving up in a fully loaded station wagon. The kids played with their cousins, and Judy shared stories and experiences with Marion and the other sisters.

Marion eventually got sick. She still came to the cottage regularly, but she didn't have the same energy for excursions. She tired easily and needed plenty of rest. Some days, she just stayed inside, wearing slippers and her pink housecoat.

One afternoon, Judy suggested a little canoe trip. Judy would paddle and Marion could just sit in the back and enjoy the sun. Marion was up for it. But they were only halfway down the path leading to the dock when Marion stopped, exhausted. She said, "I'm sorry, dear, I don't think I can do this." That's when Judy knew Marion's health was worsening.

One weekend in early fall, Bill, Judy, and their kids were up at the cottage. They were the only family there that weekend. The kids had been playing in mud in their good clothes, and Judy was doing some washing using the antiquated washing machine—it had four legs and a motorized wringer on top.

Out of the corner of her eye, she suddenly saw Marion come up behind her in her pink coat. Judy said, "Hello! I didn't know you were coming up." She turned to chat with her sister-in-law. But there was nobody there.

She had an ominous feeling that she knew what it meant.

Sure enough, half an hour later, the phone rang. It was one of the other sisters. "I just wanted to tell you, Marion died this morning in hospital."

Judy wasn't someone who ever believed in ghosts—"a lot of nonsense," she said. But that unexpected visit from her dead sister-in-law was one experience she just couldn't put aside. "Marion was definitely there. I think she came to say goodbye."

"I FEEL LIKE I'M FORGETTING SOMETHING."

—Fretfully Forgetful

Puzzles & Trivia

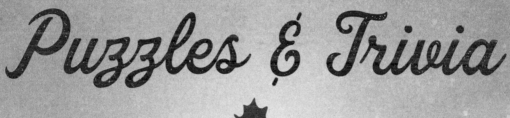

FORECASTING AND FOLKLORE

To predict weather—thunderous or serene—look for clues in nature.

TRUTH IN RHYMES

"Red sky in the morning, sailors take warning. Red sky at night, sailors delight."

"Closed in the morning . . . it'll be pouring." (Dandelions and tulips close their petals in the evening. But if they don't open them in the morning, rain may be on its way.)

"Rains before seven, fine by eleven." (If it's raining at 7 a.m., that tells you the storm is probably on its way out.)

"Open pine, weather's fine." (Pine cones are nature's hygrometers—which means they indicate humidity levels. When there's moisture in the air, they seal their seeds until it's dry outside again.)

CLOUD SIZE AND SHAPE

Mammatus clouds (puffy, with a pattern of pouches) often turn into thunderstorms.

Cirrus clouds (wispy and stringy) mean a storm or rain may follow. Those are the clouds that create a ring around the moon—a lunar halo—a sign that unsettled weather may be around the corner.

Altocumulus clouds (these look like fish scales) mean you can expect rain within a day.

The higher the clouds, the fairer the weather.

CRITTERS

Supposedly, if a cat washes behind its ears, or sneezes, or snores, it's sure to rain.

If you're sitting on the dock or around a campfire, listen to the crickets. Count the number of times a cricket chirps in twenty-five seconds. Divide this number by three and then add four. According to the cricket, that's what the temperature is in degrees Celsius. (It's best to do a few measurements and use the average.)

PUZZLES & TRIVIA

BOGGLING BUGS

QUESTIONS

1. Why do fireflies glow?

2. How small is a no-see-um?

3. Do male honeybees die after mating with the queen?

ANSWERS

1. For a variety of reasons.

2. About 1 to 3 mm.

3. Yes, they do.

Now, for some further information.

FIREFLIES, A.K.A. LIGHTNING BUGS

Fireflies produce a chemical reaction inside their bodies that allows them to light up. The main purpose of the glow is to attract a mate. Males fly around, turn their lights on and off, and hope to catch a female's attention. Studies have shown that females choose mates according to their flash patterns. (Intense flashing seems especially attractive.) The light can also serve as a warning to predators, who seem to understand that a firefly's body has an unpleasant taste.

NO-SEE-UMS, A.K.A. BITING MIDGES

Despite their name, these pests are not invisible. One authority describes the tiny bug as having "a couple of blades inside its mouth part." And no-see-ums don't occur in giant swarms. They're stealthier than mosquitoes.

HONEYBEES

Yes, that's the sole purpose in the life of a drone (the male bee)—to mate with the queen. And then it dies.

And here's some other bee trivia. It takes one colony of honeybees (about 30,000 bees) to pollinate an acre of fruit trees. A colony in early spring can have about 10,000 to 15,000 bees. A normal colony has only one queen, who may lay up to two thousand eggs per day. And to make one pound (454 grams) of honey, a bee must tap two million flowers.

VACATION VARMINTS

1. Porcupines shoot their quills—true or false?

2. How many quills does a porcupine have?

3. How do porcupines mate?

4. Frogs and toads cause warts—true or false?

5. How fast do foxes run?

6. How fast do wild rabbits run?

7. How wide do moose antlers extend?

8. How much does a moose eat per day?

9. How big, and how heavy, is a bald eagle's nest?

10. How far can an owl rotate its neck?

11. Do wolves mate for life?

12. Do raccoons hibernate?

13. Besides dams, what do beavers build?

14. Are skunks polygamous?

15. What do skunks eat?

16. What do you call a group of skunks?

17. Is spraying a skunk's first line of defence?

18. Are some people unable to detect a skunk's spray?

19. Do coyotes make different howling sounds?

20. How far does a coyote's howl extend?

FLIP THE PAGE TO FIND OUT THE ANSWERS...

PUZZLES & TRIVIA

ANSWERS TO "VACATION VARMINTS"

1. False. Porcupines don't shoot their quills. (But the quills detach easily.)

2. About 30,000 quills per porcupine.

3. Very carefully.

4. False. Frogs and toads don't cause warts, although the skin of toads has a warty texture. Frogs, on the other hand, have smooth skin.

5. Up to 50 km/hour. (By comparison, Usain Bolt's world record is 44 km/hour.)

6. About 35–45 km/hour.

7. About 1.5 metres.

8. About 20–25 kg (and moose eat only plants).

9. A bald eagle's nest, or aerie, can range from 1.8 to 2 metres in diameter and weigh more than 1,000 kg.

10. An owl can rotate its neck up to 270 degrees.

11. An estimated 3 to 10 percent of mammals are monogamous—and wolves are among this group. Wolves are believed to be very affectionate to their mates and are especially close to each other after mating.

12. Raccoons don't properly hibernate, and they stay active all year round. However, especially in northern areas, they nap in their dens for several weeks at a time.

13. Beavers are the engineers of the natural world. They build not only dams but also canals, sometimes linking one pond to another. Beavers also know how to control the direction in which a tree will fall.

14. Male skunks are polygamous and may mate with several different females each mating season. After mating, the male leaves the female, taking no part in raising the young.

15. Skunks prefer insects and grubs (killing 70 percent of types of insects considered harmful to humans), but skunks are omnivores and eat a wide variety of plant and animal matter. Immune to snake venom, they are even known to eat poisonous snakes like rattlesnakes.

16. A group of skunks is called a surfeit.

17. When threatened, skunks release a powerful smell through their anal glands. But they really prefer not to and will first try other approaches—growling, spitting, fluffing their fur, shaking their tail, and doing a little warning dance.

18. About one in a thousand people are immune to the smell of skunks.

19. Coyotes make a variety of sounds: greeting sounds (low-frequency whining), growls, lone howls, and group howls.

20. Howling sounds can travel almost a thousand metres. (Their purpose is to identify who's howling and what their gender is.)

LANDMARK CABINS

SAM MCGEE'S CABIN
Whitehorse, Yukon

There are strange things done in the midnight sun
*   By the men who moil for gold;*
The Arctic trails have their secret tales
*   That would make your blood run cold;*
The Northern Lights have seen queer sights,
*   But the queerest they ever did see*
Was that night on the marge of Lake Lebarge
*   I cremated Sam McGee.*

Sam McGee was an unsuccessful prospector from Ontario who went to the Yukon and became known as the Roadhouse King. His name became immortalized in Robert Service's great poem "The Cremation of Sam McGee." The building is a one-room log cabin with a frame gabled roof. According to many, it was built by McGee in 1899. The cabin now stands in the yard of the MacBride Museum of Yukon history in Whitehorse.

GREY OWL'S CABIN
Ajawaan Lake, Prince Albert National Park, Saskatchewan

This cabin is associated with the naturalist Archibald Belaney, commonly known as Grey Owl, and his tame beavers. Grey Owl, who promoted and publicized conservation practices, gained international fame through his wildlife writings, films, and lecture tours. The animals were a part of his home, and the cabin is also known as the Beaver Cabin.

MAUD LEWIS PAINTED HOUSE
Art Gallery of Nova Scotia, Halifax

Maud Lewis overcame the physical challenges of rheumatoid arthritis to become one of Canada's most famous folk artists. In the little house that would become known as the Maud Lewis Painted House, "Maudie" painted on every surface she could find—walls, mirrors, wallpaper, and household items such as breadboxes and a cast iron stove. As a tribute to the artist, who died in 1970, a group of citizens from the Digby, Nova Scotia, area launched a restoration project, later taken over by the Art Gallery of Nova Scotia. Almost all the furnishings on display are original to the house. The interior has been restored to how it looked in the mid-1960s.

BEER UP HERE

Cenosillicaphobia: *noun, the fear of having an empty beer glass.*

The most popular alcoholic beverage in Canada is beer, which makes up more than 45 percent of all alcoholic beverage sales in the country.

The first commercial brewery in Canada was built by Jean Talon in Quebec City in 1668. That factory survives today, known as the Talon Vaults, in the lower city of Old Quebec.

In 1786, John Molson established his first brewery in Montreal. Alexander Keith & Son founded their brewery in Nova Scotia in 1829. John H. Sleeman established his first brewery in St. David's, Ontario, seven years later. Then, in 1840, Thomas Carling opened his Brewing & Malting Company in London, Ontario, soon followed in the same city by John Labatt's. In 1867, Susannah Oland began brewing October Brown Ale and opened the Army and Navy Brewery—now Moosehead—in Nova Scotia. Moosehead is Canada's oldest, and largest, independent brewer.

According to *Beer Advocate*, forty-six of Canada's top one hundred beers were brewed in Quebec, twenty-five in British Columbia, thirteen in Ontario, six in Alberta, four in Manitoba, four in Nova Scotia, and two in the Yukon.

Canada ranks eighteenth in the world when it comes to annual beer consumption per person—53.5 litres.

CHOCOLATE BARS
YOU WON'T FIND
SOUTH OF THE BORDER

The average consumption of chocolate in Canada is 6.4 kilograms per year, or 160 bars of chocolate per year, per person, which makes us the ninth-largest consumer of chocolate in the world. That's one kilo more than the United States. Maybe that's because you won't find these favourites south of the border:

Aero
Big Turk
Caramilk
Coffee Crisp
Crispy Crunch
Crunchie
Glosette
Maltesers
Mr. Big
Smarties
Wunderbar

PUZZLES & TRIVIA

ANSWERS (TO "CAN YOU NAME IT?"): 1. LAKE OF THE WOODS; 2. MACDONALD LAKE; 3. BRAS D'OR LAKE;

4. THE KAWARTHAS; 5. THE SUNSHINE COAST; 6. MUSKOKA; 7. GEORGIAN BAY; 8. CAVENDISH BEACH

CAN YOU NAME IT?

One person can be the quiz master and read these descriptions to their cottage crew to see whose body of knowledge about bodies of water is full-bodied. The answers are on the facing page (244).

1. CAN YOU NAME THE LAKE?

Located in Northwestern Ontario, this lake's name may sound generic; however, the scenery is anything but. If you visited one of the lake's islands each day, it would take you almost forty years to finish your tour. It is easy to see why the lake's Ojibwe name is Pikwedina Sagainan, the "inland lake of the sand hills." In fact, the lake's English name may be a mistranslation of this more descriptive moniker. The area surrounding this lake is the nesting habitat of piping plover, and the lake itself is home to many species of game fish, most notably muskie. There is evidence that this lake has been inhabited by Indigenous Peoples for over eight thousand years; they lived closely connected to the land and water, hunting game, fishing for sturgeon, and cultivating wild rice in shallow waters. Can you name the lake?

2. CAN YOU NAME THE LAKE?

Ontario's Haliburton Highlands is home to a remote lake with a window into Canada's ancient past. Submerged in the lake is a massive stone structure, initially thought to be left behind by long-melted glacial ice. Upon closer examination, an underwater archaeologist discovered that the cairn was in fact constructed by the ancient Indigenous inhabitants of the area, likely as a route marker for hunting or fishing. Later in the lake's history, the Indigenous Peoples used another method for marking trails: *shiwaakii*. Indigenous children would climb to the tops of young trees, which bent under their weight, leaving crooked trunks at the correct path. Eventually the First Peoples began intentionally tying down saplings to create these markers. If you know where to look, you can still find distinctive 4- or H-shaped trees near the lakes of the Haliburton Forest and Wildlife Reserve. Perhaps you can even spot one at this lake if you look carefully. Can you name the lake?

3. CAN YOU NAME THE LAKE?

An internationally recognized UNESCO biosphere reserve, this "lake" is really a saltwater estuary, where fresh water meets the ocean to create a unique habitat for fish and wildlife. It is also one of the rare places where the Trans Canada Trail becomes a waterway and hiking gives way to paddling of all varieties. But hiking can still be found here on the trails of Goat Island. There, the Eskasoni First Nation has established interpretive panels and art installations to share their culture and history as the largest Mi'kmaw community in the world. The name *Eskasoni* comes from the Mi'kmaw word *we'kwistoqnik*, which means "where the fir trees are plentiful." Certainly, there are many fir trees alongside this lake—whose Mi'kmaw name is Wjinene'n Pit'upoq—on Cape Breton Island. Can you name the lake?

4. CAN YOU NAME THE LAKE CHAIN?

Resting on the jointure of Paleozoic limestone and Precambrian granite, this chain of lakes boasts some of the earliest sites of human habitation in Ontario. First Peoples have been living throughout this lake chain for over 12,000 years, likely settling here shortly after the great ice sheet began to melt. Known in English as Peterborough, the area was called *Nogojiwanong* by the Ojibwe people, meaning "place at the end of the rapids." Paddling is still a popular pastime in this chain of fourteen connected lakes, with peak season falling between May and October. The chain's most commonly used name is a Wendat (Huron) word meaning "bright waters and happy lands," popularized by tourism promoters to draw more business to the area. Can you name the lake chain?

5. CAN YOU NAME THE COAST?

This 180-kilometre stretch of coastline in British Columbia is accessible only by ferry, boat, or plane. All road access is blocked by the bordering mountains. This creates an isolated paradise for travellers who are respectful of this home of the skwxwú7mesh, shíshálh, Tla'amin, Klahoose, and Homalco Nations. Their rich cultures and languages have been present in the area for thousands of years, with stone tool artifacts discovered in the region that date to more than 10,000 years old. The skwxwú7mesh (Squamish) people had no written language system prior to the mid-1960s. The written system that was developed uses a 7 to represent a glottal stop, a slight catch in the throat that separates the sounds preceding from those that follow. The shíshálh people, who speak another Coast Salish language, have recently helped restore two official place names in the area to their Indigenous roots: the community of ts'ukw'um and the waters of skelhp. Can you name the coast?

6. CAN YOU NAME THE LAKE DISTRICT?

This lake district is synonymous with cottage country in Ontario, containing 1,600 lakes. It is part of the traditional territory of the Anishinabek peoples, which include the Ojibwe, Odawa, and Potawatomi Nations. Together they are known as the Three Fires Confederacy. The most commonly used name for the district may have come from the name of an Ojibwe leader with the meaning "not easily turned back in the day of battle." The terrain in the area is quite rocky, as it sits on a portion of the Canadian Shield. Some rocks from the area have been dated as more than 1.5 billion years old, which means they may have been part of the earth's earliest crust. Seasonal visitors and tourists have been drawn here since the late 1800s, when the railway first reached the region. It was also home to Canada's first tuberculosis sanitorium. Can you name the lake district?

7. CAN YOU NAME THE BAY?

Although it is often called the sixth Great Lake, that's a misnomer, as this body of water is actually connected to Lake Huron. It is more commonly referred to on its own because it is sheltered from the rest of the lake by Manitoulin Island and a peninsula. The bay is located on Anishinabek territory, and its Ojibwe name is Mnidoo Gamii. In 2020, its traditional name was incorporated into the UNESCO biosphere reserve name of the area. It is home to the world's largest freshwater archipelago, also known as the Thirty Thousand Islands. This unique mosaic of land and water supports more than a thousand distinct habitat types, home to diverse species of birds, mammals, reptiles, and amphibians. The reserve is partnered with local First Nations, not-for-profits, and municipalities to conserve over fifty at-risk species, such as the bald eagle and monarch butterfly, in the Maamwi Anjiakiziwin Initiative. Can you name the bay?

8. CAN YOU NAME THE BEACH?

Found on stunning Epekwitk, also known as Prince Edward Island, this beach is part of a resort district on the northern shore. The Mi'kmaq, First Peoples of the Island, call the area Pemamkiaq, which means long sandbar. The beach lives up to its name, with long sandy stretches that are one of the most popular destinations in Prince Edward Island National Park. The area also draws tourists more interested in literary history than sun and sand. The park is home to the Green Gables Heritage Place, the inspiration for L.M. Montgomery's classic Canadian novel series *Anne of Green Gables*. Every year, thousands of tourists visit the area during the summer to enjoy beaches, golfing, and lobster dinners. Can you name the beach?

PUZZLES & TRIVIA

TIPS AND TRICKS FOR YOUR COTTAGE

KEEP COOKIES CRISP

Separate soft cookies from crisp ones when you store them. Otherwise, the crisp cookies will become soft.

NO MOULDY CHEESE!

Wrap a few cubes of sugar in with your cheese—it will help prevent mould.

FRESH EGGS!

Test the freshness of an egg by dropping it in water. If it sinks, it's fresh.

REMOVING CORN SILK

Dampen a paper towel and brush downward on the cob of corn. Every strand should come off.

SPEED UP THE KETCHUP

Insert a drinking straw into the ketchup bottle, push it to the bottom of the bottle, and then remove the straw. There should now be sufficient air to start an even flow.

IS AN EGG HARD-BOILED?

Spin it. If it twirls round and round, it's hard-boiled. Raw eggs wobble and won't spin.

BUTTERING UP YOUR CORN

Rub a hot cob of corn onto a slice of buttered bread.

HOT POTATO!

Keep baked potatoes warm by slipping them into an oven mitt.

SOMETHING SMELLS FISHY (YOUR HANDS, FOR EXAMPLE)!

Moisten your fingers and dip them in salt before handling fish. You'll find that it lessens the odour. Even better, the fish won't slip and slide out of your hands while you prepare it.

FRESH MARSHMALLOWS

Marshmallows won't dry out if you keep them in the freezer. Separate them with scissors when ready to use.

SPILLED RAW EGG ON THE KITCHEN FLOOR?

Sprinkle some table salt on the spilled egg, wait fifteen minutes for it to soak in, and then use a broom to sweep the egg off the floor.

BATHROOM MIRROR IN A FOG?

Here are two ways to prevent a bathroom mirror from fogging up. The potato method: slice a potato in half and rub the exposed surface against the glass. The shaving cream method: smear shaving cream on the mirror and then wipe it off with a clean cloth.

BITS OF BROKEN GLASS EVERYWHERE?

Pick them up by pressing a few slices of bread over the shards. Be sure to throw the bread away.

PET HAIR ON FURNITURE?

Put on a rubber glove and rub off dog or cat hair.

UN-DAMPEN A CLOSET

Place a box of chalk on a shelf—it will help remove the moisture.

GREASE STAIN REMOVAL

Pour club soda over the stain, rubbing it in gently. Baby shampoo sometimes works, too.

FRUIT JUICE STAIN REMOVAL

Sprinkle some salt on the stain and then rinse the item in cold water. Now wash it in warm water using liquid detergent.

SPLINTER REMOVAL

Remove a splinter by applying a paste of baking soda and water. Wait several minutes for the splinter to emerge. No digging required!

GET LINT OFF A CARPET

Slide six to eight elastic bands, evenly spaced, around the surface of a cardboard paper-towel roll. Roll the contraption up and down your carpet in rows. The lint and fluff will get caught up in the gaps between the elastic bands.

MINTY TOILET BOWL CLEANER

Pour a small cupful of mouthwash into the toilet bowl. Wait fifteen minutes, dip a toilet brush in the water, and quickly wipe the surfaces. One flush later and the stains are gone.

PREVENT RUNNY SOAP

Place a strip of aluminum foil on the bottom of a bar of soap to prevent the messy scum from getting all over your sink or tub.

ONE GOOD TURN

Remember which way to turn a knob: left is loose, and right is tight.

REMOVING CHEWING GUM FROM CLOTHING

Place the garment in a plastic bag and put it in the freezer. Wait at least two hours and remove clothing. Scrape off the frozen gum.

FRESHEN UP YOUR LUGGAGE

Save old bits of soap, place them in a mesh bag, and leave the bag in your suitcase to prevent a musty smell.

PEST CONTROL: ANTS

White pepper or fresh or dried sage helps repel ants. Or leave salted cucumber peelings where ants congregate.

BROWN PATCHES ON LAWN COURTESY OF A PUPPY?

Restore the green to your grass by pouring some beer on the patches. The fermented sugars in the beer will act as a natural fertilizer.

SILLY ANSWERS TO SILLY QUESTIONS

These are said to be real questions that international tourists have asked Canadians, along with some snappy answers from armchair rhetoricians. Why not try creating your own?

Are there supermarkets in Toronto, and is milk available all year round?
No, we hunt and gather all our food. And milk is illegal.

I have never seen it warm in Canada. How do the plants grow?
We import fully grown plants—and then we sit around and watch them die.

Will we be able to see polar bears in the street?
Depends on what you've been drinking.

Which direction is north in Canada?
Face south, then do an about-face.

When I insert my card into a Canadian bank machine, does it give me Canadian money?
Yes, but only Canadian Tire dollars.

What time do they turn on the northern lights?
About an hour after they turn off the southern lights.

How do they get Lake Louise to turn blue?
They add hundreds of bottles of mouthwash. You'll notice it smells nice and minty too.

Where do you live all winter?
We hibernate in caves, of course.

I want to walk from Vancouver to Toronto. Can I follow the railroad tracks?
Of course you can—it's only 4,400 kilometres. Bring lots of water.

CANADIAN FOOD

How well do you know your Canadian culinary creations?
Test your knowledge with the following questions to discover your ranking.

1-3 CORRECT: CANADA GOOSE
4-6 CORRECT: MAPLE SYRUP MOOSE
7-8 CORRECT: TRUE POUTINE-EATING CANADIAN

1. What do you call a flattened doughnut without a hole?

2. Which three-layer dessert square has a graham-cracker crumb base, custard filling, and melted chocolate? (Hint: It's named after a city in British Columbia.)

3. What is the name of lean pork loin that's been brined and rolled in cornmeal?

4. Which drink made with Clamato juice, vodka, and Worcestershire sauce comes in a glass with a salted rim?

5. What do you call a pastry containing ground pork? (Hint: It's a traditional part of Christmas celebrations in Quebec.)

6. Which beverage-flavoured chocolate bar is hard to find outside Canada?

7. Which small pastry has a tour trail of eighteen bakeries devoted to it in Wellington North, Ontario? (Hint: It's baked with a filling of butter, sugar, syrup, and egg.)

8. What is the most-purchased pack aged grocery item in Canada? (Hint: The Canadian nickname for this pantry staple resulted in an official name change in 2015.)

ANSWERS: 1. BEAVER TAIL; 2. NANAIMO BAR;
3. PEAMEAL BACON (A.K.A. CANADIAN BACON);
4. BLOODY CAESAR; 5. TOURTIÈRE; 6. COFFEE
CRISP; 7. BUTTER TART; 8. KD (KRAFT DINNER)

TIM HORTON'S TRIVIA

How well do you know our beloved deliverer of double-doubles?
Test yourself or a friend to discover your ranking.

1–3 CORRECT: TIMBIT TAKER
4–6 CORRECT: DOUBLE-DOUBLE DOWNER
7–8 CORRECT: ROLL UP THE RIM WINNER

1. True or false? Canada has the second-highest number of doughnut shops per capita in the world.

2. If you bought a small Tim Hortons coffee and a muffin every day, about how long would it take to spend $500?

3. How many billion cups of coffee does Tim Hortons sell each year?

4. Where did Tim Hortons open its first store?

5. When Tim Hortons opened its first store, how many cents was a cup of coffee?

6. When Tim Hortons collaborated with Canadian singer Justin Bieber, which treat resulted?

7. How old are Timbits? (Hint: They share a birth year with Canadian actor Ryan Reynolds.)

8. Why did the original Tim Hortons logo feature four doughnuts?

ANSWERS: 1. FALSE (WE'RE NUMBER ONE); 2. FIVE MONTHS; 3. TWO BILLION; 4. HAMILTON, ONTARIO (IN 1964); 5. TEN CENTS; 6. TIMBIEBS; 7. FORTY-SEVEN YEARS OLD (IN 2023); 8. ONE FOR EACH OF CO-FOUNDER TIM HORTON'S DAUGHTERS

HOCKEY TRIVIA

How well do you know Canada's national winter sport?
Answer the following questions correctly to take your title.

1-3 CORRECT: PEEWEE PUNDIT
4-6 CORRECT: MIDGET MARVEL
7-8 CORRECT: BIG-LEAGUE BRAINIAC

1. Where was the first organized indoor hockey game played in Canada?

2. How many National Hockey League teams did Wayne Gretzky play for?

3. Who was the first hockey player to sign a million-dollar contract?

4. How do you properly measure a hockey stick? With skates on, it should reach to a player's eyes, nose, mouth, chin, or throat?

5. Who was the youngest National Hockey League captain to win the Stanley Cup?

6. About how many thousand points did Wayne Gretzky score in his career?

7. Who was the first professional hockey player to score five hundred career goals?

8. How many faceoff spots are on a hockey rink?

ANSWERS: 1. MONTREAL (AT THE VICTORIA SKATING RINK, IN 1875); 2. FOUR (EDMONTON OILERS, LOS ANGELES KINGS, ST. LOUIS BLUES, NEW YORK RANGERS); 3. BOBBY HULL; 4. CHIN; 5. SIDNEY CROSBY; 6. ALMOST 3,000 (2,856 TO BE PRECISE); 7. MAURICE "ROCKET" RICHARD; 8. NINE

CANADIAN WATERS

How familiar are you with our freshwater fantasyland?
Test your knowledge with the following questions to claim your title.

1-3 CORRECT: PUDDLE JUMPER
4-6 CORRECT: RAPID RUNNER
7-8 CORRECT: FRESHWATER AFICIONADO

1. Which body of fresh water do Canadians just call "the Lakehead?"

2. What is the name of the river that connects Lake Superior to Lake Michigan?

3. What are the two largest waterfalls in Canada by volume of water?

4. What is the longest river in Canada?

5. Which bodies of water does the St. Lawrence River connect?

6. Which body of water boasts Canada's strongest current?

7. The Forks in Winnipeg marks the confluence of which two rivers?

8. What percentage of the world's fresh lake water can be found in Canada?

ANSWERS: 1. THUNDER BAY, ONTARIO; 2. THE ST. MARYS RIVER; 3. NIAGARA FALLS, ONTARIO, AND VERMILION FALLS, ALBERTA; 4. THE MACKENZIE RIVER; 5. LAKE ONTARIO AND THE ATLANTIC OCEAN; 6. SEYMOUR NARROWS IN THE DISCOVERY PASSAGE, BRITISH COLUMBIA; 7. THE ASSINIBOINE AND RED RIVERS; 8. ABOUT 18 PERCENT

CANADIAN GEOGRAPHY

How much do you know about Canadian geography and our place on the globe? Challenge yourself with these questions to discover your ranking.

1-3 CORRECT: MAP MILQUETOAST

4-6 CORRECT: CARTOGRAPHY CONNOISSEUR

7-8 CORRECT: GEOGRAPHY GENIUS

1. True or false? Copenhagen, Denmark, has the same approximate latitude as Calgary.

2. True or false? Canada has the longest coastline of any country in the world.

3. Which national park is Canada's largest? (Hint: It's larger than Switzerland.)

4. At which eastern Canadian border crossing do you drive south when entering Canada?

5. What is the highest mountain peak in Canada?

6. What is Canada's southernmost point?

7. True or false? Manitoulin Island is the world's largest freshwater island.

8. True or false? Florence, Italy, has the same approximate latitude as Toronto.

ANSWERS: 1. FALSE; 2. TRUE (CANADA HAS 202,080 OF THE WORLD'S TOTAL 1,162,306 KILO-METRES); 3. WOOD BUFFALO NATIONAL PARK, NORTHWEST TERRITORIES; 4. DETROIT, MICHIGAN-WINDSOR, ONTARIO; 5. MOUNT LOGAN, YUKON; 6. MIDDLE ISLAND, ONTARIO (IN LAKE ERIE); 7. TRUE; 8. TRUE

PROVINCES & TERRITORIES

How much do you know about Canada's provinces and territories?
Answer the following questions correctly to earn your title.

1-3 CORRECT: CONFEDERATION CADET
4-6 CORRECT: PROVINCIAL PUZZLER
7-8 CORRECT: TERRITORIAL TUTOR

1. What is the largest Canadian territory by area? By population?

2. Which Canadian province produces the most wheat?

3. Which was the last province to join Confederation?

4. Which province is a "Bluenoser" from?

5. What is the largest Canadian province by area? By population?

6. Which province is famous for having red soil?

7. In which province can you find the town of Gimli and its annual Icelandic heritage festival?

8. In which province can you find both the world's largest artificial mushroom and the first UFO landing pad?

ANSWERS: 1. NUNAVUT BY AREA AND NORTHWEST TERRITORIES BY POPULATION; 2. SASKATCHEWAN (ROUGHLY 41 PERCENT OF NATIONAL PRODUCTION); 3. NEWFOUNDLAND, NOW NEWFOUNDLAND AND LABRADOR (1949); 4. NOVA SCOTIA; 5. QUEBEC BY AREA AND ONTARIO BY POPULATION; 6. PRINCE EDWARD ISLAND; 7. MANITOBA; 8. ALBERTA

TOWNS & CITIES

How familiar are you with the quirks of smaller communities across Canada? Test yourself to find out how you score.

1-3 CORRECT: TOWN TOURIST
4-6 CORRECT: VILLAGE VISIONARY
7-8 CORRECT: HAMLET HERO

1. In which Canadian town is the world's longest covered bridge located?

2. One of the world's largest displays of dinosaurs is found in the Royal Tyrrell Museum, which is in which Canadian town?

3. Which Canadian town has been battling a community in Norway for the tallest moose statue in the world?

4. Wreck Beach is a popular clothing-optional beach located west of which Canadian city?

5. Which Canadian city has earned the nickname "Cowtown"? Which one is "Hogtown"?

6. What is the largest city in the Atlantic provinces?

7. Where in northern Newfoundland can you find the reconstruction of three Norse buildings?

8. Which community is known as the polar bear capital of the world?

ANSWERS: 1. HARTLAND, NEW BRUNSWICK; 2. DRUMHELLER, ALBERTA; 3. MOOSE JAW, SASKATCHEWAN; 4. VANCOUVER, BRITISH COLUMBIA; 5. COWTOWN IS CALGARY, AND HOGTOWN IS TORONTO; 6. HALIFAX, NOVA SCOTIA; 7. L'ANSE AUX MEADOWS NATIONAL HISTORIC SITE; 8. CHURCHILL, MANITOBA

CANADIAN WEATHER

You can take the heat, you can take the cold, but can you take the trivia questions? Read on to find out how you score.

1-3 CORRECT: SILLY STRATUS

4-6 CORRECT: SAVVY CIRRUS

7-8 CORRECT: CLEVER CUMULONIMBUS

1. On February 3, 1947, the small village of Snag in the Yukon hit a record –63 degrees Celsius. That's roughly the same temperature as the surface of which other planet in our solar system?

2. What place in Canada has recorded the hottest temperature (46.1 degrees Celsius)?

3. What is the average number of daylight hours in Inuvik, Northwest Territories, in January?

4. While snow accounts for only 5 percent of precipitation worldwide, that figure is considerably higher in Canada. How much of Canadian precipitation is snowfall?

5. What is the sunniest city in Canada, with the highest annual average amount of sunshine?

6. Which Canadian province or territory has never recorded a tornado?

7. Which two provinces experience the most frequent and severe hailstorms?

8. Which province or territory experiences the most damage from flooding, in dollars per affected residence?

ANSWERS: 1. THE SURFACE OF MARS; 2. LYTTON, BRITISH COLUMBIA (ON JUNE 27, 2021); 3. ZERO; 4. 36 PERCENT; 5. ESTEVAN, SASKATCHEWAN; 6. NONE (TORNADOES HAVE BEEN RECORDED IN EVERY PROVINCE AND TERRITORY IN CANADA); 7. SASKATCHEWAN AND ALBERTA; 8. YUKON (ALTHOUGH QUEBEC EXPERIENCES THE MOST COSTLY DAMAGE OVERALL)

FAMOUS CANADIANS

How well do you know our celebrated citizens? Test your knowledge with the following questions to find out how you measure up.

1-3 CORRECT: DISTINGUISHED PERSONS DABBLER
4-6 CORRECT: PAPARAZZI POOH-BAH
7-8 CORRECT: WHO'S WHO HEAVYWEIGHT

1. Who was the first Canadian to walk in outer space?

2. Who was Canada's first female astronaut?

3. The song "Honey, I'm Home" was written by which Canadian singing sensation?

4. On which denomination of Canadian bill does civil and women's rights activist Viola Desmond appear?

5. Who was the first Canadian female solo singer to reach number one on the U.S. charts?

6. Which Canadian prime minister said, in a bid for the federal election in 2007, "[We] are saving for our kids' education. And I have actually cooked them Kraft Dinner—I like to add wieners."

7. Which Canadian comedian starred in both *Bruce Almighty* and *The Truman Show*?

8. Which Canadian athlete was the first figure skater to land a ratified quadruple jump in competition?

ANSWERS: 1. CHRIS HADFIELD; 2. ROBERTA BONDAR; 3. SHANIA TWAIN; 4. TEN-DOLLAR BILL; 5. ANNE MURRAY; 6. STEPHEN HARPER; 7. JIM CARREY; 8. KURT BROWNING

QUIRKY CANADIANA

How well do you know the weird and wacky side of Canadian history?
Challenge your trivia tidbits with the following questions to claim your title.

1-3 CORRECT: FLUNKER OF FRIVOLITIES
4-6 CORRECT: MASTER OF MINUTIAE
7-8 CORRECT: TITAN OF TRIVIA

1. This building in Ottawa was the city's main jail for more than a century. Inmates included murderers along with those imprisoned for drunk and disorderly conduct. Today it is a hostel, complete with Wi-Fi. What is it called?

2. Which of the following was *not* invented in Canada: the antigravity suit, the electric hairdryer, or five-pin bowling?

3. True or false? In Halifax, taxi drivers must wear socks and cannot wear T-shirts.

4. Which of the following was *not* invented in Canada: the TV dinner, instant mashed potatoes, or the Java programming language?

5. True or false? Until 2009, it was illegal to whistle in the street in Petrolia, Ontario.

6. Which of the following was *not* invented in Canada: the green garbage bag, the retractable beer carton handle, or the lint and fuzz remover?

7. True or false? In Medicine Hat, Alberta, you cannot decorate a silo.

8. Which of the following was *not* invented in Canada: the caulking gun, French toast, or the steam foghorn?

ANSWERS: 1. THE NICHOLAS STREET GAOL; 2. THE ELECTRIC HAIRDRYER; 3. TRUE; 4. THE TV DINNER; 5. TRUE; 6. THE LINT AND FUZZ REMOVER; 7. FALSE; 8. FRENCH TOAST

REBUS PUZZLES

The next few pages are made up of visual riddles known as rebuses. In these puzzles, the arrangement of the letters and symbols suggests a common word or expression. For example, this combination

COVER

GOING

suggests "going undercover"
(the word GOING is under the word COVER—literally).
Turn the page to see how many you can figure out.

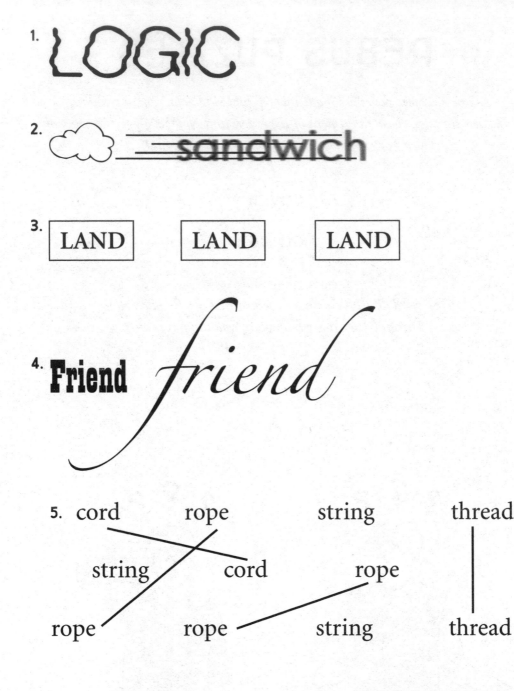

1. LOGIC

2. 🌥 ~~sandwich~~

3. LAND   LAND   LAND

4. **Friend** *friend*

5. cord   rope   string   thread
string   cord   rope   thread
rope   rope   string   thread

1. **THE SHOT DARK**

2. LOCK

KEY

KEEP

3. **G O S**

I

T

4. **TO THE CHASE**

5. **E**

SHR A IEK

R

1. ACCUSED

_____

2. HE**A**RT

3. SPEECH **LESS**

Morning
4. Noon
Evening
Night

5. F A R &

COUSIN

1. COUSIN

2. *RAZOR*

3. POWER THRONE

4. BROTHER

5. LEARNING

1. MSSEGAES

2. H
   U
     N
       T

3. PRESSURE
   ─────────
   WORK

4. B
   WATCH

5. CLOUD CLOUD
   HEAD CLOUD
   CLOUD CLOUD

1.
eyebrow eyebrow   eyebrow   eyebrow

2. LONG STOR

3. PROM ISE   PR O MISE   P RO MIS E

CREEK

4. PADDLE

5. |R|E|A|D|

"NOTES, OR IT DIDN'T HAPPEN."
—Lakeside Legacy

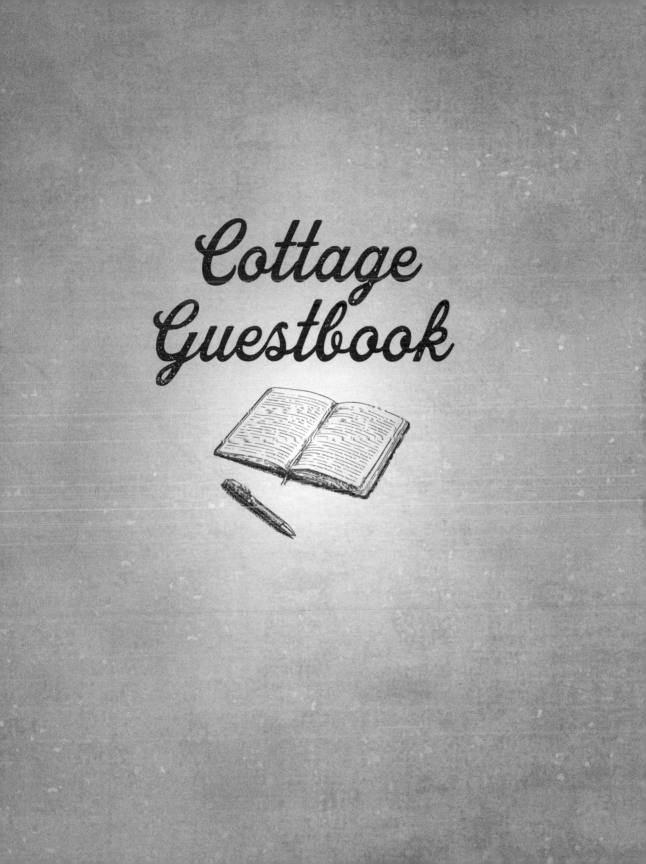

Cottage
Guestbook

PLEASE LEAVE A NOTE ABOUT YOUR VISIT TO THE COTTAGE.

WHAT WAS YOUR FAVOURITE MOMENT? BEST MEAL?
MOST SURPRISING SIGHTING OR DISCOVERY?
BIGGEST BUG-BITE TALLY? WHO ATE THE MOST S'MORES?
ANY LEGENDARY GAME WINS?
(DON'T FORGET TO INCLUDE THE DATE!)

273

COTTAGE GUESTBOOK

279 COTTAGE GUESTBOOK

COTTAGE GUESTBOOK

285   COTTAGE GUESTBOOK

COTTAGE GUESTBOOK

289 COTTAGE GUESTBOOK

ACKNOWLEDGEMENTS

We would like to thank the amazing contributors who helped make this book a reality: Duncan McKenzie, Dan Liebman, Zanne Stachura, Patricia MacDonald, Brad Wilson, and Julia McDowell. Some of you raced up to the cottage to do firsthand research for this book, and it shows (in the best way). Your punny titles, goofy games, fascinating facts, and great stories make this book the treasure trove that it is, and we thank you to the cottage and back.

ACKNOWLEDGEMENTS

We would like to thank...

A NOTE ABOUT THE TYPE

The title font used throughout this book, as well as on the front cover, is called True North—very fitting, we thought. It's vintage inspired and features fun banners, animals, symbols, and conveniently, maple leaves.

The body font is Adobe Caslon, originally created in 1722 by William Caslon, and used widely—even by printer Benjamin Franklin. The font was later revived by designer Carol Twombly, who studied samples printed by Caslon to eventually merge formerly separate fonts into the OpenType Pro version available today.